FINDING YOUR CHILD'S WAY ON THE
AUTISM SPECTRUM

FINDING YOUR CHILD'S WAY ON THE
AUTISM SPECTRUM

DISCOVERING UNIQUE STRENGTHS, MASTERING BEHAVIOR CHALLENGES

DR. LAURA HENDRICKSON

MOODY PUBLISHERS
CHICAGO

All Scripture quotations, unless otherwise indicated, are taken from *The Holy Bible, English Standard Version*. Copyright © 2000, 2001 by Crossway Bibles, a division of Good News Publishers. Used by permission. All rights reserved.

Scripture quotations marked AMP are taken from *The Amplified Bible*. Copyright © 1965, 1987 by The Zondervan Corporation. *The Amplified New Testament* copyright © 1958, 1987 by The Lockman Foundation. Used by permission.

Editor: Pam Pugh
Interior Design: Ragont Design
Cover Design: Maralynn Rochat
Cover Photos: puzzle—iStockphoto; boy—photography by Deanna Rochat
Author Photo: Mark Ross Photography

Library of Congress Cataloging-in-Publication Data
Hendrickson, Laura.
    Finding your child's way on the autism spectrum : discovering unique strengths, mastering behavior challenges / Laura Hendrickson.
        p. cm.
    Includes bibliographical references.
    ISBN 978-0-8024-4505-6
    1. Autism in children. 2. Parents of autistic children. 3. Autistic children—Family relationships. I. Title.

RJ506.A9H437 2009
618.92'85882—dc22   2008027482

This book is printed on acid free recycled paper containing 30% PCW (Post Consumer Waste) and manufactured in the United States of America by Bethany Press.

All Web sites listed herein are accurate at the time of publication but may change in the future or cease to exist. The listing of Web site references and resources does not imply publisher endorsement of the site's entire contents. Groups and organizations are listed for informational purposes, and listing does not imply publisher endorsement of their activities.

We hope you enjoy this book from Moody Publishers. Our goal is to provide high-quality, thought-provoking books and products that connect truth to your real needs and challenges. For more information on other books and products written and produced from a biblical perspective, go to www.moodypublishers.com or write to:

Moody Publishers
820 N. LaSalle Boulevard
Chicago, IL 60610

1 3 5 7 9 10 8 6 4 2

Printed in the United States of America

To Eric,
Thanks for allowing me to tell our story.
I'm so proud of you! It's an honor to be your mother.

And to Dan,
In gratitude for the sacrifices you made for Eric.

Contents

Foreword

IT IS EXCITING to see this much needed book come to fruition. Dr. Laura Hendrickson is not only a very qualified writer on her subject, but also a committed Christian and a personal friend of our family. Having had the privilege to consult with her about counseling situations involving children who were ASD, I know that her expertise and biblical perspective will be very helpful to many.

Most often, parents pray for a healthy or "typical" child. It can be concerning when God has a more challenging, and yet more perfect plan in mind. For such a time, there is Exodus 4:11 with the lessons of God's perfect wisdom and sufficient grace. When Moses was complaining about his physical limitations, God said, "who makes man's mouth, or the deaf or the mute . . . is it not I ?", implying that He is far greater than these limitations and has a great purpose in them. This book goes a long way in assisting parents to whom God has ordained one of His special children.

Finding Your Child's Way on the Autism Spectrum will help the reader to understand the varying degrees of symptoms and the individuality of each child. Taking her cues from the apostle Paul, Dr. Hendrickson stresses the importance of considering both the spiritual and physical (or "outer man" and "inner man") aspects of the child (2 Corinthians 4:16–18). She is the first to admit that there are still some mysteries to the autism puzzle, but offers that there is a great deal that parents of children on the spectrum should know and can do. Using her medical, parental, and theological backgrounds, she walks the reader through some very practical help and hope, regardless of where one's child may fall on the continuum.

Laura's experience with and commitment to raising her own son is one of her greatest assets in her mission to help other parents. Her first-hand experience offers great identification and encouragement. Her many personal illustrations let the reader know that she truly understands the ups and downs of parenting an autistic child. That understanding allows her to give realistic ideas for progressing development and addressing the autism spectrum child's heart and behavior.

This is a book of resources. Our author points strongly to the Scriptures as the greatest resource for "the inner man," offering wisdom, hope, and many practical principles concerning the autism challenge. She also gives many other resources a parent can tap into for help. Though some of the organizations she cites may not be Christian organizations, they can, with caution, offer valuable assistance with the "outer man" issues.

God can grace each parent with what is needed to faithfully parent the child He has placed in their care. He no doubt desires to grow the parents as well as help them care for and model Christ to their child. Though He is not obligated to "fix" every child, He will use many things to assist those parents who acknowledge and look to Him. Clearly, this book is one of His gracious gifts for those who need to know more about the autism spectrum child and how to give them the best chance, as Dr. Hendrickson puts it, *to soar.*

—Dr. Stuart Scott
Associate Professor of Biblical Counseling
Director, Center for Biblical Counseling
The Southern Baptist Theological Seminary

CHAPTER 1

In
HIS WAY

"Lord, I believe that You can do anything.

Please make Eric soar."

I'VE LOVED THE OLD children's movie *Dumbo* for many years.

Dumbo is a little elephant with enormous ears. In fact, his ears are so big that he trips over them all the time, producing all kinds of problems. Dumbo is mocked about his ears and snubbed when his clumsiness embarrasses the other elephants. But one day Dumbo discovers that his ears are large enough to act as wings. Upon realizing that Dumbo can fly, his only friend cries, "The very things that held you down are going to carry you up!" As the movie ends, Dumbo is rich, famous, and admired by all, performing in the circus as "the world's only flying elephant."

I remember watching the movie when Eric was a newborn. Sympathetic tears rolled down my cheeks as the other elephants ridiculed Dumbo. Couldn't they see that he was beautiful? His big ears were just *different*, not ugly! I would sing the lullaby that his mother sang in the movie to my own adorable baby, little knowing that this movie would become more than just a story to me in a few short years.

Three years later Eric, by now diagnosed with autism, became fascinated with Disneyland's Dumbo the Flying Elephant Ride. Every time we went to

Disneyland we had to ride it over and over. In those days the ride had a motto painted on its top, "Believe—and Soar." As we rode again and again I'd pray, "Lord, I believe that You can do anything. Please make Eric soar."

> *"The very things that held you down are going to carry you up!"*

I bought Eric an enormous stuffed Dumbo for his bed. He never cuddled it, but sometimes I did, and prayed again that Eric would one day soar, like Dumbo. I also prayed that one day he'd smile, he'd speak, he'd cuddle stuffed animals, and most important, that he'd tell me that he loved me. And do you know what? One day he did all of these things. In fact, the first unprompted sentence Eric ever spoke, at age four, was "I love you, Mommy." God has been so good to me!

One day Eric soared, too. I sobbed with joy as I listened to him give the valedictorian address at his high school graduation. (You can read his address in appendix C.) His top-ranked university recently announced that his GPA placed him in the top 5 percent of students in his college. It seems that the sky is the limit for the young man who was once a mute, unsmiling little boy with vacant green eyes.

I've thought about Dumbo many times since the summer when we rode the Dumbo ride over and over again. In the following years, as Eric struggled to learn to ride a bicycle, understand the concept of team sports, or make friends, he was often ridiculed, and I remembered Dumbo tripping over those ears. I sometimes cried myself to sleep, singing the little lullaby to myself.

> Baby mine, don't you cry,
> Baby mine, dry your eyes.
> Rest your head close to my heart,
> Never to part, baby of mine.
> Little one, when you play,
> Don't you mind what they say.
> Let those eyes sparkle and shine,
> Never a tear, baby of mine.

From your head to your toes,
You're so sweet, goodness knows.
You are so precious to me,
Cute as can be, baby of mine.[1]

BORN TO FLY

One day I realized that the reason Dumbo tripped over his ears was because he wasn't born to be a *walking* elephant at all. Dumbo was born to *fly*. As I understood this, Dumbo's story became a parable for Eric's life. I began to pray that his challenge might one day turn out to be the source of a unique ability, just as Dumbo's had.

Like Dumbo, Eric often didn't meet the expectations of other adults or his teachers. He was teased and sometimes rejected by his peers because of his differences. His doctors talked about his "neurological deficits" as if the essential truth about Eric was that he was lacking necessary qualities, which had to be made up somehow if he was going to have a meaningful life. But the essence of what made Dumbo himself didn't lie in what he was *unable* to do. Dumbo would never have flown if his ears hadn't been long enough for him to trip over in the first place. The tripping was a necessary stage in his development into the elephant he was born to be. He was never defective or inferior. He was just embarked upon a different path, born for a different kind of life.

I believe that this is true for all of our autism spectrum[2] children. Granted, their differences will probably keep most of them from becoming rich or famous one day. But each one is unique, and the contribution that each makes to our world will be, like Dumbo's, *because* of their uniqueness, not in spite of it. This is true even if their main contribution is in teaching the rest of us the joy that comes from loving and caring for those who cannot care for themselves. Because this is so, our focus as parents must be on so much more than simply trying to help our children be more like everyone else's.

If Dumbo were a child today, his loving mother may have arranged for plastic surgery to make his ears look more like the other elephants'. But if she had, Dumbo would never have made the distinctive contribution that he was born to make. Please understand that I'm not saying that we should just leave our autism spectrum children as they are, and not work to equip them for the most functional and rewarding adult life they are capable of. As you'll learn, I committed myself to finding all the assistance I could to help Eric to become all that he was born to be. But because I am a Christian, I also believe that God had a purpose in making Eric just as he is, and that my role is not primarily to "fix" him, but to help him realize his full potential as the unique individual he was born to be. Come to think of it, isn't this our role with our *typical* children, as well?

WHAT IS GOD'S PURPOSE FOR HIS LIFE?

I don't see Eric's challenges primarily as the consequence of a genetic mistake, a birth accident, or a vaccine injury, although any one of those things may indeed have happened to him. But the Bible teaches that his body was designed and the course of his life planned in detail by his loving heavenly Father, long before I ever dreamed of having a son. So if he did indeed suffer brain damage during his birth or from a vaccination, this, too, was from the hand of God, who is in control of all of the circumstances of our lives.

> For you formed my inward parts;
> You knitted me together in my mother's womb.
> I praise you, for I am fearfully and wonderfully made.
> Wonderful are your works; my soul knows it very well.
> My frame was not hidden from you, when I was being made
>   in secret, intricately woven in the depths of the earth.
> Your eyes saw my unformed substance; in your book were written,
>   every one of them, the days that were formed for me,
>   when as yet there were none of them.
>   PSALM 139:13–16

We are told in Romans 8:28 that "for those who love God all things work together for good, for those who are called according to his purpose." This means that everything God allows in the lives of believers (and their children) is designed by God for their benefit. This precious gospel truth ministered comfort to my heart during the dark early years when I struggled to believe that God was doing good things in our lives, even though I couldn't see them yet.

COOPERATING WITH GOD'S PURPOSE

Once Eric was diagnosed with autism I hit the books, seeking to understand as much as I could about how he was different so I could help him grow to his fullest potential. I studied the Bible too, looking for principles that would direct me as I sought to "bring [him] up in the discipline and instruction of the Lord" (Ephesians 6:4). I left my psychiatric practice and joined Eric in his early intervention program, learning techniques for teaching him language and other skills. I also prayed like crazy, asking God to show me principles from medical science and the Bible that would teach me to help him become all that God created him to be.

Life was pretty chaotic at first! But slowly, order began to emerge from the chaos. Our mute preschooler, who tested in the moderately retarded range at his first assessment, grew slowly in his understanding and use of language. His IQ score rose, too. Our obsessive little boy learned to accept the word no and turn from what fascinated him to obey our instructions. Our anxious preteen, who would become hysterical when he couldn't control what was going on around him, slowly grew in the fruit of the Spirit *self*-control. Our angry teenager slowly grew to understand that God designed his body the way He did for a reason, and to believe that His plans for his future were good, even as he struggled with the desire for acceptance and understanding from his peers.

Jeremiah 29:11 says, "I know the plans I have for you, declares the Lord, plans for wholeness and not for evil, to give you a future and a hope." God proved the truth of this Bible promise as Eric grew. He not only ministered increasing wholeness to Eric, He also brought increasing wholeness to me. I've learned so much from this journey. My goal in writing this book is to share what I've learned with others who are on their own journey.

TRAIN UP A CHILD IN HIS WAY

How did I go about helping Eric to become all that he was created to be? How did order begin to emerge from the chaos of autism? I began with what I believe is a fundamental biblical principle for child rearing, which I've found applies equally to challenged and to typical children. (See the glossary for an explanation of "typical.")

Proverbs 22:6 says, "Train up a child in the way he should go [and in keeping with his individual gift or bent], and when he is old he will not depart from it" (AMP). I like the Amplified Bible's version of this verse because it captures the intent of the original Hebrew, suggesting that we are not only to train our child to do the right thing, but that the manner of our training should be consistent with his natural abilities and interests. In recognition of this nuance, some Bible scholars have rendered the first part of this verse simply as, "Train up a child in *his way*."

This verse captures perfectly the approach I believe we need to take as we seek to lead our children toward wholeness. If we can understand how our children are different, we can learn to craft a teaching approach for almost anything they need to learn. Here is an example of how this works.

THE TRICYCLE

At age three, Eric had never ridden his tricycle. He would turn it upside down and spin the wheels, or push it back and forth while watching the wheels turn, but he'd kick and scream if I tried to put him on it and push him, or told him with words how to ride it. I thought that Eric didn't want to learn to ride and only cared about watching the wheels spin. This is how many autism spectrum kids play with their trikes, and most parents leave them alone, concluding that if they don't want to ride there's no reason to make them learn.

But Eric didn't really understand how the trike worked, perhaps because all he'd ever really noticed about it was its wheels. When I would put him on it and start to push him from behind, the movement of his feet on the pedals would startle him. Unlike typical kids, he had difficulty drawing conclusions from what he observed, so he didn't connect the motion of the pedals with the trike's forward motion. And he would never have picked up how to pedal his tricycle simply by watching other kids ride. Eric had no spoken language and didn't understand what I was saying, so he had no way either to ask for help or learn from my explanations. Most spectrum children are also unwilling to try anything new. Eric fought me when I tried to teach him to ride because of these differences.

The behaviorist we hired to teach me how to work with Eric understood these things about his challenges. He explained to me that spectrum kids are able to learn skills that they can't pick up in the usual way if they are broken down into a series of smaller steps. So teaching Eric to ride a trike "in his way" would be very different from the way the average toddler begins to ride.

Eric first had to be put on the trike against his will, kicking and screaming. Some parents balk at teaching their child to do anything he doesn't want to do, and indeed, one could reasonably ask why this was a necessary thing for Eric to learn. But the behaviorist explained that once Eric could ride, the trike would give him hours of pleasure. He also told me that it was worth the effort to push Eric through his discomfort to increase his abilities, because this would teach him that he was able to learn new things. He said that although autistic kids have to be pushed to learn at first, as they experience success they become more motivated to learn and less fearful of new things.

*An autism spectrum child can be brought
to a greater sense of competence, control over
his environment, and ability to understand how
the world works through teaching him "in his way."*

Once Eric was seated on the trike, the behaviorist pushed his left foot down on the pedal, then his right, so that Eric could see that as each foot went down, the trike rolled forward a little. His screaming slowly stopped. After moving the trike slowly and jerkily forward with each depression of the pedal, the behaviorist began to alternate Eric's feet in a smooth up-and-down motion. And, oh, the joy when Eric finally "got it" and began to pedal without help, just like the other kids!

Years later, Eric told me what was going on inside him before he could ride the trike. Because he didn't have the words to ask for or understand the help I was trying to give him, he played with his trike the best way he could figure out for himself. He fought me on learning to ride, not because he didn't want to ride, but because he didn't understand that I was trying to show him how to do it. And even though it took pushing Eric through a painful scene, teaching Eric "in his way" actually set him free to do something he really enjoyed.

This story is just one example of how an autism spectrum child can be brought to a greater sense of competence, control over his environment, and ability to understand how the world works through teaching him "in his way." This basic principle can help you craft an approach to practical challenges like potty training. It can help you determine which schooling options and curriculum will best meet his needs. Applying this principle can enable you to train him to be self-disciplined in a loving and sensitive way. As you'll see, it's a very powerful key to helping your child reach his full potential.

HAPPILY EVER AFTER?

But real life isn't like the movies, is it? In the movies the clumsy elephant flies. The kid everyone made fun of grows up to be rich and famous. His parents and the girl who believed in him before he "made good" are vindicated for their faith in him. But in real life, people who are born different usually stay different, and most of them don't "live happily ever after."

So when I tell you that, like Dumbo, Eric soared, I don't want to try to sell you a fairy tale. He hasn't become "better than normal," and his peers aren't lining up to admire him and learn his secret for success. He still faces challenges in many areas of his life. But together we have blazed a unique path, Eric's way, through a very difficult childhood and adolescence. Now as he faces the future as a young adult, Eric is beginning to discover what God had in mind when He created him so very different from other people. And we also believe that God has only begun to do all the good things He's intended from the beginning, both in and through Eric's life.

NO FOOLPROOF SOLUTIONS

A number of books in recent years have offered techniques or treatments that promise to cure autism spectrum challenges. Invariably these books create a stir, as desperate parents try the latest thing. Also invariably, most wind up disappointed. This book is different. I don't have a foolproof solution to offer you. I can't promise you that if you follow the principles I teach in this book, your child will become just like a typical child. In fact, I don't even believe that Eric has become just like a typical person. Oh, it's certainly true that he's no longer autistic. But he's still different from typical young men his age—and I don't think that's a bad thing! He's on his own developmental path to becoming the man whom God created him to be, with his own unique strengths and weaknesses, just as typical young adults are.

As you come to appreciate your own child's distinctive way, your hopes may begin to change.

The Bible tells us that when we trust and obey God, He will minister increasing wholeness in our lives. This is a promise that we can take to the bank, because God is always faithful to His promises. We can expect God to slowly bring order out of the chaos of autism as we trust Him to illumine our path, and obey the principles in His Word, but this doesn't necessarily mean that our autism spectrum child will go to college, achieve independence, or even speak. But each and every autism spectrum child can glorify God as he lives by faith within the limits of the potential that God has placed in him.

I've come to understand much about autism through almost twenty years of helping my own child and others, and I believe that you can learn to understand your child better, too. As you come to appreciate your own child's distinctive way, your hopes, like mine, may begin to change. Instead of hoping that one day he'll be the same as everyone else, you may find yourself beginning to hope instead that he'll grow to be the adult whom God designed him to be, differences and all.

This book is about teaching you to help your child to do just that. It will help you to understand how your child is different, and how you can work with his nature, instead of against it. And because we are spiritual as well as physical beings, it will also teach you principles from the Bible about nurturing his spirit and drawing him into a personal relationship with Jesus Christ, from whom his true wholeness must come.

HIS OWN WAY

Parents of typical children walk a well-trodden path, worn deep by the experience of many generations and illuminated with many lights and signposts. God has called you on a different kind of journey. Wherever your child is on the spectrum, from mild to severe, he is different enough that the usual way will not work for him. You and he or she will need to blaze a new trail together. I can't show you the one true way for all spectrum children. Your child is unique, and his path will be unique, too. But I can teach you how to wield your machete to clear the brush, and I can tell you how to determine if you're going in the right direction. I can give you principles, but the exact nature of your journey is yours and your child's to discover. Let's take our first steps into understanding together, and may the Lord bless you with wisdom as we begin.

CHAPTER 2

First Steps
IN THE WAY

"I prayed, asking God to give me the wisdom
to understand what Eric really needed."

WHEN ERIC WAS a year old, we moved to a house two blocks away from beautiful Coronado Beach in San Diego. We loved walking to the beach, and our house was near "Dog Beach," the area where dogs are allowed to run off their leashes and swim in the surf. We were enchanted by the thought of Eric growing up in the water, swimming with his very own puppy. And so Coco came into our lives the following year.

Coco loved to swim! There was no peace if I didn't take her to the beach at the appointed time daily. But Eric, who'd always tolerated being on the beach before, began to resist going all the way across the broad beach to the water's edge. He kicked and screamed if I tried to take him closer in than about fifty yards.

What in the world was wrong with him? I put him down in the sand and began walking away from him as mothers do, expecting him to run after me when I got far enough away from him. But I walked farther and farther, and still he sat quietly on the sand, staring out into space. As I stood there wondering what to do next, Coco began whining. She was afraid to go down to the water's edge if she couldn't see me from where she was. This was a fine mess. I had a puppy that was afraid to have me out of her sight, and a kid who didn't seem to care how far I walked away from him, as long as he didn't have to go any farther himself! Finally I walked near enough to the water for timid Coco to be willing to swim, all the while never turning my back on my two-year-old, who was sitting placidly in the sand twenty-five yards away from me.

What in the world was wrong with me? What kind of mother leaves her child alone on the sand so her dog can feel safe as she swims? But Eric honestly didn't appear to mind this unusual arrangement at all. I mused further. What kind of mother raises a child who doesn't need her at all? I'd learned from my psychiatric training that this kind of detachment in a child could be a sign that the mother was neglectful or abusive. But I deeply loved Eric! And I was a kind and patient mother.

> *I'll never forget the moment*
> *the doctor said that it was autism.*

Suddenly I realized—what would people think? I'd left my baby alone on the beach! I called Coco, scooped up Eric, and went home. Surely things would be different tomorrow.

But the next day was exactly the same. And so was the day after that and the next. If I'd drawn a line in the sand showing where Eric refused to go any farther, it would have been in the same place every day. I finally stopped trying to go to the beach, and took Coco and Eric on long walks instead.

Soon after that day on the beach, I realized that even the truism that boys speak later than girls couldn't explain the enormous speech delay in our two-year-old. Something must be wrong with him. I took him to a specialist.

I'll never forget the moment the doctor said that it was autism. Autism! I was devastated. *It must be because I was thirty-seven years old when Eric was born,* I thought. *How could I have been so selfish as to try to conceive so late in life?* And I was not only selfish, I was stupid, because it turned out that what was wrong with Eric had been obvious to many of our friends and family who didn't have my education.

Or was it that they didn't have my denial? Had I permanently harmed our child by failing to see the obvious because it was just too painful to admit to myself? What if it was too late to do anything for him? *Could* anything be done for him?

Does this tale of guilt, denial, and crazy-making attempts to adapt myself to an impossible situation sound familiar to you? You may have never tried to take your child to the beach, but I know that if you're the mother of a spectrum child, you've experienced struggles like mine. You've tried to be a good mother, and so far nothing has worked. Maybe you've tormented yourself with questions like mine. *Is it my fault? Can I help him?*

Whether your heart was lifted with hope as you read chapter 1, or whether your response was that this won't work for you, be encouraged. I started just where you are. And you don't need answers for all the questions you have today to be able to begin helping your child in his way. You just need to start putting one foot in front of the other and take the next step. If you do so prayerfully, the Lord will begin to guide you, step by step, just as He did for me.

SENSITIVE HEARING

One of the first things we learned after Eric's diagnosis was that he had extremely sensitive hearing. This is common in autism spectrum kids. It turned out that the reason he stopped at the same spot on the beach every day was that the sound of the waves that the rest of us love became overwhelmingly painful when he got too close to the water. The poor little guy was so disorganized in his perceptions that he didn't even realize that the painful sound was coming from his ears, so it didn't occur to him to cover them with his hands.

Boy, this was hard! We couldn't go to the beach, and Eric would scream anytime things got too noisy or chaotic. I'd left my psychiatric practice as soon as he was diagnosed and devoted myself to his care, so I was home with him full time. It seemed as though he screamed constantly, and I found myself planning our life around avoiding what upset him. This wasn't good. He needed to experience some of the chaos of daily life if he was ever going to learn to master it. So as time went on I began to ask myself how I could keep him challenged while still meeting his needs for peace and order.

I found that if I could keep our trips to noisy places brief, and experimented with ways to make the noise more tolerable for him, this gradually increased his tolerance for noise and disorder. It also occurred to me that if I spoke or sang to him constantly, this might help him develop his speech, as well as his tolerance for other sounds. So I became more talkative when I was with him than I was accustomed to being. And although I have what my sister calls "the family voice" (not a good thing!), I started to sing to him.

In time I found that Eric was more likely to cooperate with an activity when singing was involved. So I made up silly songs that I sang when he had to take his vitamins or pick up his toys. "Vi-hi-ta-mi-hi-nies, Vit-a-min-ies!" I'd sing in my deepest bass voice to the tune of the Handel's "Hallelujah Chorus." Then I'd shriek, "Vitaminies! Vitaminies! Vitaminies! Vitaminies!" in a piercing soprano, sliding the spoonful of vitamin supplements dissolved in applesauce down his throat as he chortled with joy.

Eric learned lessons immediately when they were set to song, so I found songs to help him with his memory work. As he grew, I realized that he had perfect musical memory, and only had to hear any tune once to remember it forever. Eric could hear and remember accents as perfectly as tunes. He also could mimic them with amazing accuracy, a talent he first displayed when he was learning to speak. In fact, he spoke with a Liverpool accent until he was five years old! He was imitating Ringo Starr, who narrated Eric's beloved Thomas the Tank Engine stories in PBS' *Shining Time Station* television series in the late eighties.

> *What appeared to be a negative trait when Eric was a toddler slowly grew to become an area of special ability.*

Eric tells me now that during those language-learning years he was fascinated by words that were similar but not the same and thought constantly about them, trying to understand why they were different. As he grew older he became interested in learning foreign languages. He also enjoyed analyzing the fantasy languages in Star Wars movies and the Lord of the Rings books. When Eric learned that linguistics is all about language analysis, he knew that he'd found his field.

Is Eric's sensitive hearing in childhood the reason why he has such a good ear for music and language? Is he fascinated with languages because of his early memories of learning to speak? Most important, would a gift and interests like these have emerged in a child who developed more typically?

FINDING ERIC'S WAY

I believe that what appeared to be a negative trait when Eric was a toddler (sensitive hearing) slowly grew to become an area of special ability as I worked with him in his way. If I had always kept Eric in a quiet environment, he'd never have learned to cope with noise. But if I'd ignored his need for that quiet environment altogether, he'd have found the noise so disturbing that he might not have been able to learn at all. Because both of the conditions Eric needed to learn effectively were met, his too-sensitive hearing became highly discriminating hearing. I didn't do this to try to produce a language gift; I just wanted to help him overcome a tendency that would become a disadvantage if it continued into adulthood. But because I discovered the ways he learned best, he was not only able to master what had once overwhelmed him, but it became the source of a unique talent.

How did I figure all of this out? Well, it didn't just come to me suddenly in a moment of revelation. Instead, as I walked with Eric in his way, I slowly learned what worked with him, and what made coping harder for him. I read everything I could lay my hands on about autism, and tried every idea that sounded promising.

I also prayed for him, asking God to give me the wisdom to understand what Eric really needed. I believed that God would teach me, and then I just walked with Eric one step at a time along the path that He showed me. God was faithful to His promise (James 1:5). It has only been recently that I've begun to see exactly how God was causing everything to work together for good in Eric's development right from the start (Romans 8:28). How I praise Him for His gracious work in our son's life!

FINDING YOUR CHILD'S WAY

I believe that you too can learn what works best for your child and walk with him in his way. But don't be discouraged! I'm not telling you that you have to figure out everything about your child for yourself. Although I've emphasized the fact that every autism spectrum child has his own unique way, it is also true that autism spectrum kids share some common characteristics. Doctors have identified some of these traits, and have devised ways to help you minimize problems that can arise because of them. I'll be sharing some of them in this book.

*It's best to balance the
negative with much positive.*

But before we begin to discuss specific methods for helping your child at home and at school, let's first consider some general principles. These will form a foundation for the suggestions that follow later in the book. Whether you are teaching your child to clean his room, eat in a restaurant without having a meltdown, or learn spelling words, these four principles will help you to train him in his way.

Principle #1: Your Child Needs Lavish Praise and Quiet Correction

When Eric was small, I sometimes would find him alone in his room, practicing a skill that I hadn't known he'd wanted to learn. Other times I was surprised to see a new skill appear without any evidence that he'd ever tried it before. I finally realized that he was ashamed to have us see how hard it was for him to learn, so he worked on new skills in secret. He also resisted being taught new things, and tended to quit trying when he didn't pick up on something right away.

Spectrum kids can be very easily discouraged, because they don't understand the world around them the way typical children do. Your child also may feel very powerless, because he can't be a part of deciding what happens to him if he can't express himself effectively. And because much of the behavior that comes naturally to him is considered socially unacceptable, he hears the word *no* constantly.

Please understand that I'm not telling you that you should never tell your child no. Sometimes it's necessary. But it's best to balance the negative with much positive. This teaches your child that he can fail sometimes without *being* a failure.

Our behaviorist showed me that Eric would work harder and be more confident if he was rewarded for successes with extravagant praise, and quietly corrected for his mistakes. I also learned that spectrum kids often don't register quieter praise, at least at first, so my reaction had to be exaggerated for Eric to even notice it.

No matter how mundane it seems to you, or how late it is in developing, learning any new skill is a big deal for your child. She'll be motivated to keep trying if she knows that you'll get excited about her successes. On the other hand, if you keep your necessary corrections as low-key and matter-of-fact as possible, it will help her to cope with any negative feelings she has when she misses the mark.

Principle #2: Your Child Needs Gentle Pressure to Learn

At three years old, Eric didn't want to do anything but sit under the end table and pull his eyebrows out. He didn't seem to have any of the drive to learn new things that is so characteristic of typical children. But once his behaviorist taught me that I needed to keep him interacting with me and to actively prod him into learning, I began to exert gentle pressure on him to learn. The tricycle story in chapter 1 is one example of how I was taught to do this. In time Eric stopped resisting my attempts to teach him new things, and began to genuinely enjoy learning. Once he realized that he *could* learn, he even began to take the initiative and choose new skills to learn, including hard ones that he used to resist.

> *Spectrum kids are always looking for clues to help them figure things out.*

It's often said about typical children that you don't have to teach them to explore their world; they do it naturally. Not so with spectrum kids. Because they may find even a quiet environment overwhelming, they tend to withdraw and engage in activities that help them soothe themselves. Activities like Eric's eyebrow pulling, which doctors call self-stimulation or "stimming," seem to help them to calm down, but stims can take up all of their energy and attention. As a result, they may not be as aware of what's going on around them. Gentle pressure to engage in activities, even when he'd rather just stim, will increase your child's involvement with you and his ability to understand his world.

Principle #3: Your Child Needs Firm Limits and Consistency

The first time Eric bolted out into the street alone, we didn't yet know that he was autistic. I pulled him to the curb, explained that he did not have permission to cross the street alone, said he had to obey me, and disciplined him. Then I dried his tears, kissed him, and turned him loose to play. He ran straight back into the street! I explained the rule and disciplined him again. After I let him go for the second time, Eric walked to the curb and put one toe into the street. Convinced that I had the most defiant child on the planet, I told him that he couldn't put even one toe in the street, and disciplined him again. After that, he stayed out of it.

Spectrum kids almost always have some difficulty understanding what others are telling them. Lacking the means to understand instructions or to ask questions, they're always looking for clues to help them figure things out. They may even do experiments to help them discover what is expected of them. This is what Eric was really doing as he kept returning to the street. Once he understood the rule, he didn't break it anymore.

A limit is a rule that tells your child clearly what behavior is unacceptable and what will happen if he engages in it. Your child needs firm limits to help him learn self-control. Spectrum kids who will not obey have more problems in school and learn much more slowly. Life at home will also be much less chaotic if your household has firm limits and your child knows what they are.

Because your child is always trying to bring some sense of order out of the chaos that he's experiencing, a predictable environment is very important for him. If rules aren't enforced every time—and sometimes even if they are—he'll be confused. Exceptions don't trouble typical children, because they are able to understand that even if exceptions are occasionally allowed, the rule still holds. But spectrum kids may not be able to learn a rule at all if *any* exceptions are allowed.

Your child also needs the structure of a regular routine. All kids like to know what is going to happen next, but your spectrum child may not be able to recognize your household's unspoken schedule as readily as a typical child does. Because not knowing what's coming next makes her feel anxious, she may prefer a very rigid routine. In fact, if your family doesn't have a lot of rules, routines, and order, your child may even try to make her own rules and impose them on you!

A good example of this appears in the Academy Award–winning movie *Rain Man*.[1] Dustin Hoffman plays Raymond, an autistic adult, and Tom Cruise plays his brother. The story is a classic male-bonding-on-the-road tale of the brothers' car trip across the country, with a twist. Raymond has lived in an institution since childhood. Because he was not taught to cope with change when he was young, he still becomes hysterical as an adult when things are not exactly the same every day.

Raymond's insistence on following the same routine every day makes it nearly impossible for them to make any progress on their trip. He has to watch the same television show every evening at 6:00 p.m. He can only wear underwear bought at Kmart. He has to eat certain foods on certain days. He even has to have toothpicks, instead of a fork, to carry his fish sticks to his mouth. If he doesn't get these things, he melts down.

Because you'll want to regularly press your child to learn and interact, which he'll find stressful, a predictable routine will help him tolerate the necessary changes without becoming completely unglued. It's much better to make up your own routine than to end up with a child who runs his (and your) life based upon arbitrary rules like Raymond's!

Principle #4: Your Child Needs Discipleship

"The Democrats are Communists," ten-year-old Eric informed our friends Jan and Eva.

"Eric, the Democrats are not Communists," Eva corrected.

"Yes, they are," Eric insisted. "My mommy says so."

"Eric, *we* are Democrats!" Jan said, his voice rising sharply. Eric's statement seemed to him like a deliberate insult, for Jan and Eva had escaped from Poland at the end of World War II. Eric knew that Jan had been in the Polish Resistance, and that Eva had been a slave laborer during the Nazi occupation. He knew that they'd feared Communism even more than they'd hated the Nazi occupation, and had risked their lives to escape life in Poland under another totalitarian regime.

"Eric, I never said that the Democrats are Communists!" I cried in horror, my cheeks burning with shame.

"Yes, you did," Eric said. "You said that Mrs. Simpson is 'red.' Mrs. Simpson is a Democrat, and 'red' means Communist. So Democrats are Communists."

As you can imagine, I was mortified! It took quite a bit of work to persuade our dear friends that we were not closet Nazis! I was also grieved that I'd been so careless with my speech, and that this had confused my son and hurt valued friends.

I explained to Eric that I'd been "exaggerating for effect" when I teased a friend about having been "red" in college. What I'd meant was that she had been a member of the student group, Students for a Democratic Society (SDS), which had organized the campus protests in the seventies. Everyone but Eric who heard my comment had understood what I meant, and laughed.

I explained that the word *red* could be a hurtful term if it was used to refer to any American, in any way but as a joke. I told him that it actually wasn't a good word to use at all because it wasn't kind, and that I was sorry for having used it under any circumstances. I reminded him that saying that Democrats are

Communists would be particularly hurtful to Jan and Eva, not only because they are Democrats, but also because of the difficult circumstances they'd endured in their youth.

Eric responded, "It's okay to say something if it's true." This prompted another long explanation about how we don't say something even if it is true if it could be hurtful to others. It was a number of years before Eric began to understand that others have the same feelings that he does, and learned to try to put himself in another's place before he said something that could be hurtful.

Eric could be very stubborn in those early years. He had difficulty understanding humor, and could be very insensitive to others' feelings. Even though I understood that spectrum kids find it difficult to read the expressions on other people's faces and notice their reactions, his tactlessness was disturbing. Eric also found it hard to understand another person's point of view, and tended to see the truth in a very black-and-white manner. Because of these challenges, kindness came much harder for him than it does for typical kids. He would say what he thought was true whether or not it was kind or necessary, and he didn't even realize when he hurt other people. He needed to be taught to be gentle. To learn this, he first had to understand why it was as important as truthfulness. This was not something that came naturally to him.

The Bible tells us, "The fruit of the Spirit is love, joy, peace, patience, kindness, goodness, faithfulness, gentleness, self-control . . ." (Galatians 5:22–23). This means that those who are indwelt by God's Holy Spirit because of their faith in Jesus Christ will develop these character traits as they trust Him to work in their lives. This is no less true for spectrum kids than it is for typical kids.

Even children with severe challenges can grow in these areas. For Eric, natural weaknesses have begun to be transformed into character strengths as he's grown in Christian discipleship over the years. Through the work of the Holy Spirit in his life, his tendency to speak bluntly is gradually being transformed into honesty tempered by sensitivity. Rigid refusal to change is developing into loyalty, faithfulness, and reliability. Stubborn refusal to yield is becoming willingness to take an uncompromising stand for right. The tendency to believe whatever he hears is growing into a faith that stands firm in the face of the wind and the waves of a secular society.

The Bible teaches that this kind of personal transformation is the birthright of all who believe in Christ in a saving way. The Lord tempers the character weaknesses of all Christians as we mature in Him. Although this truth gives confidence to all believers, it is a source of special hope for those of us who know just how much our special children need God's power to moderate their natural tendencies. The nature of their differences may make teaching discipleship more challenging for parents, but they can't prevent this growth in grace from occurring.

An autism spectrum child may learn and develop in a different way, but he's still a human being, made in the image and likeness of God. If he's a believer, he'll reflect God's likeness more and more as he grows, even if he continues to struggle with very significant challenges. As we train our spectrum children in their way, therefore, we must never neglect the spiritual dimension of their nurture.

GOD HAS BROUGHT US A LONG WAY!

By God's grace, Eric and I have both come a long way since that awful day on the beach so long ago. Eric has grown in maturity and Christian discipleship, and I've learned to help him grow while adjusting myself to his way. I've also learned how to look to God for help with my weaknesses as a mother, and stop judging myself so harshly.

Right now you may be full of negative thoughts about your parenting skills, and full of doubts about your ability to lead your child in his way. But be encouraged! My God is your God, and He will be faithful to you as He has been to me. He'll give you wisdom, and help you grow in grace. If you're feeling inadequate, have faith! God does remarkable things through people who know how weak they are, and who look to Him for the wisdom and strength they need to do what He's called them to do.

He's called you to do one of the most difficult jobs on the planet, parenting an autism spectrum child. God always equips those He calls if they look to Him in prayer for help. So call out to Him, dear parent, and start putting one foot in front of the other. You'll find your child's way the same way I did—one step at a time!

CHAPTER 3

Shepherding the
HEART OF YOUR CHILD

"No matter how careful you are to anticipate negative behaviors, there will be times when you'll need to discipline."

SOON AFTER ERIC'S DIAGNOSIS with autism, he developed an ear infection with a high fever. After seeing his pediatrician, I took him with me to get his prescription filled. Since we were a military family and the navy offered free prescriptions, I used their pharmacy, but it was noisy and crowded. You'll remember from chapter 2 that autistic children don't deal well with crowds and noise, and sickness makes coping even more difficult. After five minutes in the pharmacy, Eric threw himself on the floor and started screaming.

I didn't know what to do. I tried everything I knew to comfort him, but I couldn't get him to stop. The only solutions I could think of were to stay in line and let him scream, or to go home without the medicine. But the doctor had said that he needed to begin taking the medicine immediately.

"I always made sure *my* children behaved in public," the woman standing behind me in line proclaimed loudly to the man behind her, avoiding my gaze as she did so. "Parents today don't know how to control their children."

My cheeks burned with shame. Before I became a mother I'd seen poorly disciplined children throw tantrums in public and had promised myself that *my* child would never behave in such a way. But now I had an autistic child who seemed to melt down for no reason, and there was nothing I could do about it.

In chapter 2, I explained that your child's differences one day might be the source of a unique calling. But an opposite truth is more likely to affect you before that day comes: difficult behavior problems develop as a result of these same differences.

PROBLEM BEHAVIORS: RECOVERY OR ACCEPTANCE?

Autism spectrum parents disagree about what to do about problem behaviors. Some see them as deficits that must be remedied so their children can fit into society better. These parents hope that science will find a reversible physical cause for their child's condition, and they pursue treatments that offer hope of a cure. Their goal is to find something that will make their child like everyone else's.

Others take the opposite tack, considering their child's condition to be unchangeable. These parents insist that their children can't help themselves and shouldn't be expected to. They work to increase society's acceptance of their child's condition so they can be accepted without having to change, as people with vision or mobility challenges are.

Both of these positions are motivated by a love that's willing to make extraordinary sacrifices for a child's well-being. It's unfortunate that these two parental camps have become somewhat polarized in recent years. The recovery group accuses the acceptance group of being defeatist or unwilling to sacrifice, and the acceptance group accuses the recovery group of not accepting their children. Are we stuck with irreconcilable differences on the subject of problem behaviors, or can we find some common ground?

WHAT DOES THE BIBLE TEACH?

The Bible doesn't leave parents of typical children in the dark about how God wants them to be raised, and its principles shed light on nurturing your spectrum child, too. I already mentioned three of these truths in chapter 1: God designed your child while he was still in the womb, He has a plan for him (Psalm 139:13–16), and the plan is good (Romans 8:28). Let's add the truth that, as a human being, your child is made in the image and likeness of God (Genesis 1:27), just as you are. This means that, in agreement with the acceptance group, there's nothing wrong with your child. God made him the way he is, and He has a good plan for his life.

> *Our spectrum kids need a*
> *Savior just as much as we do.*

On the other hand, the Bible also teaches that your child has inherited a sinful nature as a result of Adam's fall in the garden of Eden (Genesis 5:1–3), just as you have. Because of Adam's sin, he wasn't born innocent and naturally good (Psalm 58:3; 51:5). God's Word commands you to correct his behavior (Proverbs 19:18). It promises benefits for him if he is corrected and consequences if he is not (Proverbs 29:15). The Bible even says that if you love your child you'll correct her (Proverbs 13:14). In agreement with the recovery group's beliefs, these verses tell us that your child is *not* fine the way she is; she needs to change.

Of course, the Bible teaches that *we* aren't fine the way we are, either. In fact, that's the whole point: our spectrum kids need a Savior just as much as we do. Using discipline as a tool to help them grow to trust Christ is just as essential for them as it is for our typical children.

BUT MY CHILD IS DIFFERENT!

But wait, you may be thinking, *my spectrum child is different! Do the Bible's commands really apply to her the same as to my typical children?* At first glance it may seem as though this can't be so, but the Bible assures us that it is. People with various challenges are described throughout Scripture, so their presence among God's people is assumed, but the Bible's only special commands about them are not to take advantage of them (see, for example, Deuteronomy 27:18). We can therefore conclude that God has given one standard for challenged and typical people alike. And really, doesn't this make sense? Your spectrum child was born with a sinful nature, like your typical kids. She sins, the same as your typical kids (Romans 3:23). This means that she needs a Savior, just like all the rest of us (Romans 6:23). This means that she has more in common with us than we may have realized.

Our spectrum kids require the same sort of nurture that our typical ones do. They need to be taught to love and obey God, and to love others as they love themselves. Pastor Tedd Tripp refers to this nurture as "shepherding a child's heart."[1] But although the Bible doesn't exempt us from shepherding our spectrum children's hearts, the tools we use may be very different than those that work with our typical kids. This is training them up in their way—finding means to apply biblical principles to teach those who don't learn in the usual manner.

TAKING THE INITIATIVE INSTEAD OF REACTING

After breakfast, I helped three-year-old Eric down from his chair. He made a beeline for Coco, as he did every morning. I knew that once he got there, he would pull her tail hard enough to make her yelp in pain. Producing this reaction in Coco seemed to fascinate Eric somehow. Perhaps it made him feel powerful or in control, or maybe he just enjoyed the noise she made.

This sounds terrible, but remember that I mentioned in chapter 2 that spectrum kids often feel powerless. They're also fascinated by intense reactions of others and will try to reproduce an interesting noise over and over. Most important, they have difficulty understanding and relating to the feelings of others. Because of these differences, it's not uncommon for them to hurt an animal or a smaller child repeatedly, as if they don't care that they are hurting them. And they may keep on doing it even after they've been disciplined repeatedly.

If I hadn't understood these things about Eric, I'd have been shocked and horrified that he wanted to hurt Coco over and over again. But because I understood this difference, I put my focus on trying to interrupt the pattern instead of responding emotionally to it. This doesn't mean that I didn't work hard to help him understand why hurting his pet was cruel. It certainly doesn't mean that I didn't discipline him on occasions when he did manage to hurt her. But whenever I could, I tried to redirect his behavior *before* he hurt her.

When I'd see Eric heading over to Coco, I'd quickly join him and model a loving interaction with her. "Hello, Coco. That's a good girl. Goooood dog, Coco." Eric would pick it up and croon after me, "Goooood girl, Coco." Then I'd pet her, and as I saw his hand reach for her tail, I'd grab it and guide it into a petting motion. "I love the way you're kind to your dog. God wants you to be kind." I wasn't always able to redirect Eric, but I tried to make the positive times with Coco far more numerous than the times when he'd hurt her. And in time the problem behavior became more infrequent until finally it stopped.

I learned that staying close to Eric and trying to anticipate problems helped keep my interactions with him positive while he was little. Experts call this close contact "shadowing." By taking the initiative instead of always having to react to his behavior, I found that less discipline was necessary. Over time, practicing positive behaviors (and enjoying the positive attention that came with them) became more attractive to Eric than the problem behaviors had been.

CRAFTING A DISCIPLINE PLAN
FOR YOUR CHILD "IN HIS WAY"

In chapter 2, I introduced four principles your child needs:

1. lavish praise and quiet correction
2. gentle pressure to learn
3. firm limits and consistency
4. discipleship

These general principles can be used to create an approach to anything that you are trying to teach your child in his way. Let's look at how I used them to develop my plan to teach Eric not to hurt Coco. Principle #1 says that your child needs lavish praise and quiet correction. Remember that spectrum kids can be inattentive, so the praise needs to be "over the top" in intensity for them to notice to it. In fact, they'll find any communication more interesting if it's intense, and if it interests them, they are also likely to imitate it. So I used a high-pitched, exaggeratedly sweet tone of voice and repeated my praise of Coco until Eric imitated it.

Once a ritual is established with a spectrum kid, it attracts him just as strongly as the negative behavior once did, because he finds repetition comforting.

I petted Coco, and I took Eric's hand and guided it into a petting motion. If I had just told him to pet Coco, or showed him without guiding his hand, he might have ignored me or failed to understand. This is principle #2, that spectrum kids need gentle pressure to learn. When we use as many ways as possible to communicate what we want, we improve their compliance. Taking a child's hand or shoulders and "walking" him through the steps of obedience at the same time you tell him what to do will increase the likelihood that he'll understand and obey.

Then I praised Eric for being so kind to Coco (principle #1 again). I told him God wants us to be kind (principle #4). Finally, and very important, I guided him on to the next activity, moving him gently away from Coco at the end of our positive interaction with her, thus removing the temptation to hurt her by turning his attention to something new. This is principle #3, providing firm limits and consistency.

And I taught this interaction over and over again, every day. Each time Eric approached Coco, I tried to be there to replace the unkind behavior with a new one. In time the happy morning visit with Coco became a ritual, something Eric wanted to do every morning exactly the same way. Once a ritual is established with a spectrum kid, it attracts him just as strongly as the negative behavior once did, because he finds repetition comforting. Eventually Eric petted and praised Coco, even when I wasn't there to make it happen.

WHY SHADOWING IS IMPORTANT

You may be thinking that this reminds you of how you trained your typical toddler. And indeed, many of us shadowed our little ones when they first began walking. But our typical kids don't need such intense involvement for long. Our spectrum kids are different. They need ongoing help coping with their impulses and emotions, and more directive help with their behavior.

Shadowing helps you prevent misbehavior, so you'll need to discipline your child less often. This prevents the discouragement that can result from frequent failure. Reducing the frequency of negative behaviors also weakens undesirable habits. At the same time, by praising frequently you're showing her that doing the right thing makes her happy. Each time you have to discipline her for doing the wrong thing, you've missed an opportunity to show her that obeying God's commands leads to blessing (Ecclesiastes 2:26). Each time you praise her, you show her that learning from you is more enjoyable than misbehaving.

Am I suggesting that you manipulate every aspect of his life, so he never has the chance to do the wrong thing? Well, yes and no. I know that you wouldn't shadow your typical child once he was past babyhood, because he needs to learn to obey. When he chooses to disobey and is disciplined, he learns. The time will come when your spectrum child will need this experience too, once he can understand your instructions and is learning more typically. I'll discuss what's called "fading," which is removing extra helps like shadowing once your child is ready, in chapter 4.

On the other hand, some spectrum kids may not progress to the level of understanding that will enable them to manage themselves without help. If this is the case for your child, you'll want to continue to direct his environment. This is not so he can rule the home like a little tyrant, as Raymond tried to do with his rituals in the movie *Rain Man*, but so you can continue to guide him in right behavior to the extent he is able, given his challenges. This is lovingly shepherding a child who may continue to be a weak sheep throughout his life. If your child needs this kind of special help, it's nothing to be ashamed of. The Bible teaches that Jesus is our chief Shepherd (1 Peter 5:4). A precious passage tells us:

> He will tend his flock like a shepherd;
>   He will gather the lambs in his arms;
> He will carry them in his bosom,
>   and gently lead those that are with young.
>   ISAIAH 40:11

Christ's gentle care of those who, through no fault of their own, will need extra help throughout their lives, is our example.

WHAT ABOUT SPANKING?

No matter how zealously you shadow your child, and no matter how careful you are to anticipate negative behaviors, there will be times when you'll need to discipline him. But what's the best way to discipline a spectrum child? Timeouts can work with typical kids, because their social drive makes being isolated from you a real punishment. But spectrum children don't have the same social drive. They prefer isolation, so a time-out is not a punishment for them. Because they have trouble understanding, using words alone to correct behavior isn't as effective as it is with typical children—and we all know that typical kids often don't respond to verbal correction alone. So sometimes it will be necessary for you to spank. This may sound like a problem to you. It certainly was for me!

Do you remember my story in chapter 2 about Eric running into the street? You can imagine how terrible I felt after Eric was diagnosed with autism, when I realized that he hadn't understood me when I told him to stay out of the street. I'd spanked him three times for disobeying a rule when he hadn't understood it! He wasn't being defiant when he stuck his toe into the street. He was just trying to find out what the rule was. And once he did understand it, he never disobeyed it again.

It's just this sort of difficulty that may cause you to decide that you can't spank your spectrum child because you don't know if he understood the rule he broke. Your child's teacher even may have told you not to spank him for this reason. Or you may be unwilling to cause your child physical discomfort. *After all,* you may think, *he faces so many difficulties already. I just can't make life harder for him by physically disciplining him! And what will he think of me if he doesn't understand why I'm doing it?*

After I learned that Eric was autistic, I decided that I'd never spank him again. I was afraid that he wouldn't understand what I was trying to do, and would hate me for hurting him. But not spanking made things much worse. Why? *Because* he didn't understand what I was telling him!

Given that he couldn't understand what I was saying, in deciding not to physically discipline him I was also, in effect, deciding not to try to make him stop negative behaviors. But I couldn't allow him to hurt Coco, or run into the street, or bite the neighbor kids, and I couldn't always be there to prevent it. So Eric's behavior went completely out of control when I stopped disciplining him.

TAMING MY TONGUE

Not only did Eric's behavior go out of control when I stopped spanking him—mine did, too! Although I knew that he didn't understand what I said, I just couldn't seem to stop saying it anyway. But because he ignored much of what I said in a normal tone of voice, I started shouting at him. The problem was, Eric ignored me when I shouted, too. But although I wasn't changing Eric's behavior with my yelling, I *was* affecting him, nonetheless.

It was some time before I completely understood the devastating effect that shouting has on autism spectrum kids. To begin with, most of them have sensitive hearing, so listening to shouting is physically painful. Secondly, spectrum kids are frightened by any loss of emotional control in the people around them. And when they're afraid, they freeze up emotionally and lose all ability to receive new information. So when I shouted at Eric to get his attention, I was actually *decreasing* his attentiveness.

But the most important reason not to yell is that we don't want to make our children afraid of us! We want them listening to us and learning from us. And I'm afraid that I did frighten Eric with my emotional outbursts, even though they didn't occur all that often.

Finally I realized that I was hurting him more with my shouting than I would have by spanking him. I was teaching him to be afraid when he did something wrong, instead of motivating him to learn from his mistakes. I was also teaching him to fear my displeasure, instead of teaching him to please God. I'm so thankful that I finally learned that physical discipline often leaves the fewest emotional scars.

GENTLE SPEECH AND FIRM DISCIPLINE

What kind of speech is easiest for an autism spectrum child to hear when he is being disciplined? The more serious the offense, the more quiet and calm your voice needs to be, and the more slowly you should speak. I found that Eric listened best when my "you're in trouble" voice was exceptionally quiet, slow, and *low*-pitched. This is in contrast to the voice I used to try to interest him in learning something new, which was high-pitched, energetic, and enthusiastic.

Unless you have the patience of Job, you'll probably find that you're unable to correct your child using a consistently quiet, calm voice if you don't also use physical discipline, at least sometimes. In fact, a very strong reason for deciding to spank is to avoid turning into a screaming shrew! But the Bible gives us a more important reason for choosing physical discipline to shape behavior— God instructs us to (Proverbs 23:13). When I learned that God didn't except special-needs kids from His directive that children receive physical discipline, I began spanking again, and Eric's behavior came back under control. And so did mine!

Interestingly, one of the earliest researchers to work with autistic children discovered that physical discipline helps spectrum kids to become more self-controlled and teachable. It is true that many objected to his use of what he called "aversives" because they were not applied in a loving, controlled way. Today, aversives are not used in early intervention or schools because we've found that spectrum kids respond much better to praise in a learning environment. But this doesn't mean that spanking is bad for them when used lovingly to teach obedience by parents in a Christian home. Physical discipline, when used in a quiet, controlled, understanding way, is just another tool for motivating your child to become more self-controlled.

HOW TO DISCIPLINE

It's very important to discipline in the right manner if your child is to learn the right lessons from your correction. You should only spank after explaining what rule was broken. If your child has limited understanding, you may need to use very simple words, like "no hitting" to explain the rule, and use the same words to repeat the rule each time you discipline. Even Coco was able to learn to obey simple commands in this way. Your child can learn this, even if his function is very low, if you keep it simple enough.

> *A spanking should always end with coaching*
> *your child to ask God to forgive him, and*
> *with love, hugs, and forgiveness from you.*

It's important to teach only one rule at a time to your spectrum child. Trying to teach several at the same time will confuse and frustrate him. Once he's thoroughly mastered the first one, you can introduce another. It's also important to discipline for *every* instance of disobedience to the rule you're working on. If you aren't completely consistent, he may not understand what you're trying to do. Because spectrum kids are easily discouraged, this could lead to his giving up and just ignoring you. And don't forget to enthusiastically praise him each time he obeys!

A spanking should be given in a controlled way, *never* in anger. It should be done with the minimum number of swats necessary to bring about a change in his attitude. Finally, a spanking should always end with coaching your child to ask God to forgive him, and with love, hugs, and forgiveness from you. If he has limited understanding and verbal skills, your coaching can be very simple, but it should happen every time you spank. You shouldn't spank if you aren't prepared to take the time to go all the way to make the correction loving and positive.

Meltdowns are a special discipline issue. Spanking is not a good way to respond to a meltdown, because it tends to escalate rather than resolve a problem. Autism spectrum children struggle with very intense emotions, and once they're already melting down, physical discipline will make them feel even more out of control and will worsen their behavior. I'll address meltdowns in detail in chapter 6.

A child who is spanked, then lovingly led to reconciliation with God and with you will learn that she can make right what she's done wrong, and that her relationship with you doesn't have to stay broken because of her misbehavior. This is very healing and freeing for children—and for parents too! A child who is disciplined in this way will learn self-control, and your home will be more peaceful as a result.

THE SPANKING RITUAL

Do you remember that I mentioned that spectrum children are very attracted to rituals? Doing things the same way every time helps them learn. So I developed a "spanking ritual" that I used every time with Eric, never changing the order or wording of the questions and answers.[2] It went like this the year he was four:

Me: "What did you do?"
(Making sure that he knows what rule he broke)
  Eric: "Hit."
Me: "What does God say about what you did?"
(Reinforcing that God's Word is our standard for behavior)
  Eric: "No hitting."
Me: "Did you do right or wrong?"
(Making sure he understands that he's being disciplined because he did what God says is wrong)
  Eric: "Wrong."
Me: "What does God say I should do when you do wrong?"
(Making sure he understands that I'm not spanking him because he made me angry, but in obedience to God's command)
  Eric: "Spank."
Next I spanked him, then held him in my arms and comforted him until he stopped crying.
Me: "Does God forgive us when we ask?"
  Eric: "Yes."
Me: "That's right!"
(Open Bible and paraphrase) "God's Word says, 'If we confess our sins God will forgive us' (1 John 1:9). Jesus died on the cross for our sins. Because Jesus paid for our sins, God forgives us when we ask Him. Let's tell God you're sorry now."
  Eric: "Father God, I'm sorry."
Me: "Let's ask Him to forgive you."
  Eric: "Please forgive me."
Me: "Will God help us to obey Him if we ask Him to?"
  Eric: "Yes."

Me: "Let's ask Him now. *Dear Father God, please help Eric to obey Your rules next time. In Jesus' name, amen.*"
Me: "Did God forgive you?"
    Eric: "Yes."
Me: "So now God's Word says you're all clean. Let's play!"
(Big hug and kiss)

When Eric was three, I had to ask the questions and also prompt him to give the answers to the questions. By the time he was four, he could give the brief answers I've shown here. I used the ritual for many years, expanding with teaching and explanations as his ability to understand grew.

BIBLICAL DISCIPLINE YIELDS GOOD FRUIT

What is the result of consistent, biblical discipline that is focused upon reconciliation with God and restoring broken relationships? I remember one day when Eric was eight. We were at the zoo with his friend David. Eric did something wrong, and I told him that he would be disciplined when we got home.

"Can't I have my spanking now?" Eric asked.

"Are you CRAZY?!" David screamed with laughter. "Your mom might forget by the time you get home! Why do you want your spanking now?"

"I want to get right with God," Eric said calmly.

Before you get the wrong idea about my perfect child, or my brilliant parenting, I must emphasize that Eric later went through struggles with teen rebellion, just as many typical kids do. The time came when he questioned his parents' authority and said things like, "You don't understand how things are today!" But a foundation of early love for God and His Word, and consistent discipline, has enabled us to weather those storms and arrive at young adulthood with his trust in Christ intact.

CHAPTER 4

Educating the
MIND OF YOUR CHILD

"It seemed to me I could hear the angels themselves rejoicing."

IT WAS ERIC'S FIRST DAY of early intervention training. Scott, our supervising behaviorist, was seated in a toddler-sized chair. Eric stood between his legs. Directly behind Eric stood a second toddler chair, which was also positioned between Scott's legs.

"Sit down!" said Scott in a friendly, but commanding voice. Simultaneously, he gently pushed Eric down by his shoulders into the chair, and held him in place. "Great job! Good sitting! Way to go, Eric! Good obeying!" chorused Scott and the three other behaviorists in the room, clapping wildly as he popped a single M&M candy into Eric's mouth. Eric's mouth dropped open in astonishment, and then closed on the M&M with a faint smile.

Scott took his hands off Eric's shoulders, and Eric popped up out of the seat like a cork out of a bottle. "Sit down," said Scott in a matter-of-fact voice, placing him back into the seat for a second drill. The behaviorists repeated their praise and applause. "Good sitting!" Eric got another M&M. Then Scott took his hands away. Eric bobbed back up and turned to walk away. But Scott had his feet wrapped around the legs of Eric's chair. This placement kept Eric inside his legs and in front of the chair.

"Sit down." Eric shrieked in anger as Scott gently pushed him down into the seat a third time and the behaviorists repeated their enthusiastic chorus. Scott kept him in between his legs and repeated the trial over and over, praising Eric for his "obedience" at the end of each repetition. This went on for fifteen minutes. Then Scott said, "Take a break," and moved his legs to let Eric leave the chair. Eric fled into my arms and clung to me until the end of the five-minute break.

Then Scott placed him back between his legs for another round of training. More instructions, more praise, and more M&Ms followed. Eric stopped screaming in response to being instructed to sit, but he didn't obey the directive on his own.

At the end of the second break, Eric was once again placed standing between Scott's legs. "Sit down," came the now-familiar instruction. And wonder of wonders, Eric sat, all by himself! The room erupted in celebration, with shrieking and wild clapping. Scott popped three M&Ms into Eric's mouth, held his arms over his little head in a victory posture, and tickled him. Eric crowed with joy. It seemed to me that I could hear the angels themselves rejoicing. Although Eric didn't know what the words "sit" or "down" meant, he now knew what "sit down" meant, and he also knew that obeying had made him very happy!

TEACHING A NONVERBAL AUTISTIC CHILD

Applied Behavioral Analysis, or ABA, is one method for teaching language and other skills in the autism spectrum child's way. The "sit down" drill is always the first one mastered. This is because learning that disobedience is not an option and that obedience produces praise is the basis for everything else that follows. Once Eric understood that he had to obey every instruction Scott gave, without exception, he was ready to learn other skills, each of which was based upon obeying a direction.

As time went on I began to notice a change in him. He started to enjoy the drills.

"Touch cat," Eric would be told, and then his hand was placed on a picture of a cat. Applause always followed, along with praise: "Good touching!" After being physically prompted to touch the picture a number of times, Eric understood that the animal in the picture was called "cat," and would touch it himself when directed.

"Say cat," Scott would instruct. "Cat," he would add immediately in a louder voice. The repetition of the word was a prompt for Eric, showing him what Scott wanted him to do. Once Eric understood that "say" was a direction to speak the word it was associated with, he would give the response without the prompt.

At first, Eric resisted when forced to "work" like this. Left to his own devices, he would have crouched under the coffee table and stimmed all day long. But as time went on I began to notice a change in him. He started to enjoy the drills. And he was more attentive and noticed more, even when he wasn't working on drills.

Eric began to enjoy the praise he received even more than the M&Ms. In fact, he continued to work for praise even when the candy was offered less often (this is known as "fading" the reward). He also started to use the words he'd learned in the drills to ask for things, in the process discovering that being able to use words is rewarding for other reasons besides getting praise or candy. And, most wonderfully from my perspective, the obedience he learned in his drills transferred to his behavior in our everyday life.

After Eric had learned enough nouns, we taught verbs and even adjectives and adverbs. He began speaking in sentences. As time went on, we also taught him numbers and letters. He learned to sort, compare, and categorize objects, and to follow two-part, then three-part, instructions. His ability to pay attention increased as he worked to master progressively harder skills. Eventually we taught him how to participate in elementary conversations, and to play games that typical kids his age liked. This gave him the ability to begin connecting with others.

In time it was no longer necessary to reward Eric with candy at all. Even later, we didn't need to reward him with enthusiastic praise. Why? Because he'd discovered the satisfaction from doing a good job, a sense of competence from pleasing me, and the joy of learning.

WHY DOES EARLY INTERVENTION WORK?

I believe that ABA, and behavioral programs like it, are effective because they're consistent with biblical principles, even though they aren't intentionally Christian interventions. In the Bible, God Himself uses rewards and penalties to teach His people to obey as they learn what it means to follow him.[1] In fact, the principle that obedience leads to blessing, and disobedience leads to God's discipline is found throughout both Testaments.

We've already discussed how God commands us to train our children using positive and negative consequences (Proverbs 7:2; 8:32; 29:15). Without a foundation of attentiveness and obedience toward authority, no child could learn. Behavioral techniques improve spectrum kids' attentiveness and teach obedience in a way they can understand. As your child progresses in his early intervention program, he'll also learn the basic preschool skills he'll need to be ready to start school.

You'll find that as your child's behavior and understanding improve, he'll need these techniques less and will begin to respond to more typical child training methods. And so as he develops, you'll want to make sure that you adapt the way you deal with him to reflect his improving abilities. You wouldn't discipline a typical five-year-old the same way you would a one-year-old. Parents of typical children modify their training as their kids grow in obedience and understanding, and it's important to do the same with your spectrum child as he develops. Just as with your typical kids, you should do your best to ensure that your discipline reaches your child's heart, so that ultimately he does the right thing because he wants to please his heavenly Father, rather than just to gain a reward or avoid punishment.[2]

Prior to the discovery of ABA, there was no way to teach a nonverbal autistic child to understand his parents' words. I am so grateful to God for providing the techniques that taught Eric to understand our language! It was the foundation for everything that has followed. I'll discuss how to choose the right early intervention program for your child in appendix B.

WHAT COMES AFTER EARLY INTERVENTION?

What if your child wasn't diagnosed until he was already beyond the preschool years? Well, in some ways that's a good thing! It was already obvious when Eric was two years old that there was something seriously different about him. This means that he was much more severely affected than a child who is first recognized as challenged when he starts to school. If your child was identified later, he probably doesn't need to learn as many of the foundational skills that early intervention provides.

But he probably hasn't acquired all of these skills, and this makes missing the early intervention years at least a potential problem. That's because uneven development is a hallmark of autism spectrum disorders. Generally speaking, lower-functioning children are delayed in most aspects of their development. But higher-functioning kids can be ahead of schedule in some areas, while remaining seriously behind in others.

For example, your bright kid with Asperger syndrome may be highly verbal and read far above grade level, but may lack the ability to comprehend much of what she reads. She may be able to solve algebraic equations, but unable to follow a simple, three-step instruction like, "Go upstairs to my dresser, get the scissors from the top drawer, and bring them to me." She may find noise and disorder extremely unpleasant, and respond to surprises by melting down. She may not yet ride a bike, or be able to follow the ball when her class plays soccer at recess.

HOW YOU CAN HELP YOUR SCHOOL-AGE CHILD

If your child has these kinds of difficulties, either because he was diagnosed later or because his early intervention didn't address them, you'll want to find ways to help him acquire these skills and others like them. You can't rely on the school to teach your child all he needs to learn, even if he's full-time in a dedicated special education classroom. His teachers will naturally emphasize academic skills and the kinds of behaviors that will help him to learn at school, but won't be primarily concerned with whether he can clean his room, catch a ball, or cope with change at home.

Fortunately, it's possible to use modified behavioral techniques to teach new skills at home. Don't worry; I'm not saying that you need to design your own early intervention-style drills! But you *can* use behavioral principles to help him develop new abilities. For example, you can teach complex skills one step at a time, in easy-to-learn pieces, then put the pieces together. This is similar to the way that Scott taught Eric to ride his tricycle, as described in chapter 1.

Another helpful technique is shadowing. I introduced shadowing in chapter 3 as a means of helping a small child learn to obey. If your child is older and higher functioning, you won't want to be following him around all day managing his environment the way you would with a toddler or preschooler. But this doesn't mean that shadowing him sometimes won't continue to be helpful. Instead of watching him all the time, you can be standing by to give extra help only when you anticipate that he may find a particular situation overwhelming.

This is growing in your understanding of his unique way.

49

This might mean helping an older child develop the ability to respond to three-part instructions by prompting him to remember each step in sequence. It might mean talking your child through a complex task in advance to break it into easier pieces for him. You may find that you need to stay beside him at a birthday party to help him interpret what is happening and prompt him to give proper responses. *Now Peter is going to open your present. He likes it! Say: "I'm glad you like it." Say: "You're welcome."*

But it's also important to recognize that spectrum children can become too dependent upon their helpers, because they don't have as strong a desire to develop independence as typical kids do. So you'll want to balance your shadowing with fading. This entails slowly removing the extra support a little bit at a time and watching for your child's reaction. If he panics, you've removed too much, or perhaps you've removed a reasonable amount, but too soon. Should he not handle the change well, you can restore all the help, or some of it, tailoring your support to meet his need. If you're careful to remember both that he needs extra assistance, and that you don't want to make him too dependent, you'll learn to balance these two concerns in your child. Once again, this is growing in your understanding of his unique way.

"ERIC, PLEASE CLEAN YOUR ROOM"

There was nothing more likely to provoke a meltdown in Eric in the early years than the simple request that he clean his room. This wasn't because he was lazy or wanted to have a messy room. In fact, "disorderly" was a word that Eric often used to describe anything he didn't like. A lack of order wasn't just unattractive to Eric, it was intolerable!

But Eric had difficulty deciding where to begin a big job and how to carry it through to completion. He also had trouble choosing where each toy should go. He'd learned basic techniques for categorizing objects in his early intervention, but it was hard for him to apply this skill to the *specific* problem of sorting the toys in his room. So Eric needed help to grow in his ability to successfully break down a big job into smaller pieces and address each small piece correctly.

> *My continued availability kept him from getting frustrated, but a little distance promoted independent thinking.*

When he was five I needed to be there with him every moment to tell him, step by step, what to do next, breaking down the job into manageable steps. So I'd say, "First pick up all of your cars and trucks and put them in the red bin," and wait till he'd finished that task. "Now pick up all of your trains and track and put them in your train box," and wait again. At this stage, I didn't ask him to make any decisions for himself, because he was overwhelmed enough simply by the prospect of tackling such a big job.

By the time Eric was seven, I'd begun to fade my step-by-step directions, and I did so by prompting him to make some decisions himself. I'd ask, "What do you need to do first?" Eric would answer, I'd agree, and he'd do it. If he wasn't sure what to do, I'd ask more questions as prompts, until he came up with a first step. When he was done with that first task, he'd ask me what he should do next, and I would answer, "What do you think needs to be done next?" And so on. I found that if I wasn't there to ask him what the next step should be, it didn't occur to him to ask himself. But if I was there to prompt him, he was able to progress from one step to the next without being told exactly what to do.

The year Eric was nine, he was able to tell himself what to do without my prompting him. At this point, I tried to stay out of his room while he was working, because if I was there he tended to rely on me rather than think for himself. I only came into his room if he asked a question, and I left as soon as I'd dealt with it. My continued availability kept him from getting frustrated, but a little distance promoted independent thinking.

When Eric was ten, he could clean his room without any help from me, except when he'd acquired new belongings that didn't fit into categories he already had. When this happened, I'd talk him through the task of classifying a new possession by asking, "What is this used for? Do you have anything like it?" If he didn't have any items that were similar, I'd ask him questions to help him decide for himself where would be a good place to store it.

I'll never forget Eric coming to me as a young teenager to tell me that his room, although not messy, had become "disorderly," so he'd reorganized it all by himself in a completely new way. What a thrill it was to see Eric acquire the ability to make independent organizational decisions—a skill that even some typical teens never develop!

WHAT KIND OF SCHOOL IS BEST FOR MY CHILD?

Although you'll be teaching your child many life skills in this manner, she'll also need to attend school. As always, it'll be important to carefully consider her way as you make the crucial decision of which school to send her to. She'll have her own unique pattern of strengths and weaknesses, and these will help you determine what type of school will best enable her to achieve her highest potential.

Eric's Educational Way

Eric had improved remarkably during his two years of ABA. He'd attended preschool with a shadow for much of that time. But I'd noticed that, in spite of his shadow's diligent efforts to fade her assistance, Eric was easily overwhelmed by the noise and activity of even a quiet, well-regulated preschool classroom. He would stim constantly when left alone. He didn't really listen to the teacher when she spoke to the group, although he did sit quietly and wasn't a behavior problem. But if his shadow didn't repeat back to him what the teacher had just told the class, he didn't register it. If the shadow didn't get him started, he wouldn't even notice that the class was doing a project, let alone do it by himself.

And yet he could learn very quickly if the teacher got down on his level, looked him in the eyes, and engaged his attention. I didn't have a lot of confidence that he would do well in a typical kindergarten classroom because of his attention problems. Would he do better in a different kind of school?

I liked many of the features of Montessori schools, and especially their emphasis on each child having a unique developmental path. But I knew Eric needed that gentle pressure to learn. Montessori programs let a child set his own educational goals, relying on his inner drive to master new things. But Eric tended to avoid activities that he found difficult. The Montessori philosophy said that he would tackle these activities when he was "ready," but I wasn't sure that his reluctance was a readiness issue. Because change made him very anxious, I didn't feel confident that he was going to seek out new challenges without that gentle pressure.

On the other hand, I had concerns about regular public and private schools too. Their emphasis on teaching skills based upon the child's grade, rather than on his ability, seemed a bad fit for a child with uneven development. Eric was way ahead of schedule in some areas, but still relatively delayed in others. And his poor attention when not shadowed suggested that he wasn't going to be successful in a regular classroom.

Having visited our local public school's special education classroom, I wasn't comfortable with his being placed there either, since most of the children in the classroom where he'd be were slow learners, and he was testing very bright. Autistic kids are notorious imitators, and I worried that Eric would begin imitating behaviors he saw in the special ed classroom that I'd worked hard to prevent or eliminate during the early intervention years. I also wanted to ensure that he didn't imitate the slower learners and fail to move forward as quickly as he was able to do.

Believing it was best overall for our family, we finally decided to homeschool Eric. He thrived on directive, one-on-one contact with me, and I was able to provide him with the quiet and order he craved. I waited until I was sure that he was ready to master an academic skill before I introduced it, and this protected him from unnecessary frustration. But I also kept up the gentle pressure I knew he needed to keep trying new things and moving forward. Because he wasn't anxious at home with me, his stims and obsessions decreased, and over time disappeared altogether. I gave him the freedom to begin studying languages at age ten. He loved to do "kitchen science" experiments, and he worked three years ahead of grade level in math. Homeschool was a good fit with Eric's way.

> *I'm convinced that every adult did the best they could, but Eric, like Dumbo, was hurt by the taunts of some of his peers about things that he didn't have the power to change.*

But although Eric thrived academically, I failed to realize that he wasn't getting all of the different kinds of social experience that he needed. He did participate in many activities, but in retrospect it was not enough. Eric began Christian school when he was twelve, skipping a grade because he did so well on his placement tests. But it was a very difficult transition for him.

I'm not sure how we could have made a better school decision than the one we made. But even if our decision was the best possible one, Eric's years at the Christian school were far from ideal. Skipping a grade made him the youngest child in his class, but he was still bored much of the time. Yet he was much less able to organize his time and keep track of his assignments than were his classmates. He was also very young for his age in terms of his interpersonal skills, and probably would have had social problems even if he'd been placed several grades lower.

We'd chosen a very small Christian school, with a staff that was committed to helping him succeed, but it was difficult for some of the teachers to understand why Eric was so advanced in some areas while so delayed in others. This sometimes led to misunderstandings. They really worked to help Eric fit in, but unkindness and lack of acceptance were still frequent occurrences among his classmates. I'm convinced that every adult did the best they could, but Eric, like Dumbo, was hurt by the taunts of some of his peers about things that he didn't have the power to change.

Your Child's Educational Way

All this points to the fact that there are no perfect solutions for children who are so different. The school decision is just one more example of why you need to understand as much as you can about your own child's way in order to make the best choice possible for him. Let's check out some of the factors you'll consider as you make your decision.

If your child is low functioning, as Eric was at the start, he should begin as a preschooler in a high-quality early intervention program. How he responds to this will help you determine the best course for his primary schooling. Did he develop good communication and attention? He might do very well in a full inclusion classroom. Indeed, studies have shown that some "graduates" of ABA programs need no special educational support to succeed in regular school from kindergarten onward.[3] On the other hand, many autistic kids will continue to have difficulties with communication and attention. For them, homeschooling or a special education classroom may be the best options.

If you think you have a bright child, but ongoing challenges merit his placement in an autism special education classroom, you may want to seriously consider homeschooling, as we did. By homeschooling, you'll be able to tailor his education to his specific strengths and weaknesses. And if he socializes mainly with typical kids, you won't have to worry that he'll pick up new stims or obsessions from other kids at school.

On the other hand, if your autistic child has not developed the ability to speak or is showing signs of being a slower learner, you may want consider the special education classroom. If he needs lots of speech and occupational therapy, the school can integrate these special services with his classroom work. If he has other medical issues, like cerebral palsy, a multicap (multiple handicap) classroom will have nurses and trained teachers who are experts in teaching the physical skills he'll also need to learn.

You could still homeschool. Spectrum kids who aren't progressing in their special education classroom sometimes come home for their schooling, and many have improved.[4] But this choice isn't practical for all families. If you have several children, or if your child has other medical issues, you may find that what he requires is too much for you to manage alone. In cases like this, the public school special education classroom may meet a real need.

If your child is diagnosed with Asperger syndrome around the time he begins school, he'll probably be placed in an inclusion classroom, perhaps with pullouts for speech therapy or other programs. Many Christian schools will also try to accommodate an Asperger child, if he is able to work at grade level. But some "Aspie" kids won't pay attention well in an inclusion classroom, and you may find yourself spending hours on tutoring and homework during his after-school hours. Homeschooling may seem an attractive alternative to hours of struggle over homework after school every day, if this is the case.

Your child may have serious problems with peer relationships from the early grades on, or these may develop as he approaches the middle school years. I'll be discussing relationship problems in detail in chapter 7, but for now let's just look at how these issues may affect your school choice.

Schools vary greatly in the types of resources they have available to help different children fit in. You may find Christian schools to be very willing to devote effort to peer problems, but they may have fewer resources to devote to your child's needs. Public schools can vary widely. One may have many available resources, but a too-tolerant attitude toward bullying. Another one may have a very strict "zero tolerance" policy toward bullying, but lack the resources your child needs. If you're fortunate enough to live in a community that has a private school dedicated to autism spectrum disorders, or even one that specializes in learning disabilities, it will offer special assistance with relationship issues, perhaps even as a formal part of its curriculum.

No Perfect School

But in most cases, you'll probably find that the perfect school for your child doesn't exist, so you'll need to supplement whatever isn't being addressed during her school day at home. This will probably include practical life skills, but it may also require tutoring and other services. On the other hand, if you decide to homeschool your spectrum child, you'll want to be especially alert to the danger of failing to adequately address her social development. Homeschooling through high school probably isn't a good idea for verbal kids who'll need to learn how to confront social issues sooner or later.

TRUSTING GOD WITH YOUR CHILD'S WAY

Are you feeling a little overwhelmed right now as you hear about all of these options, none of which are ideal? How can you ensure that your child's teacher will understand him as you do? How can you protect him from unkindness?

You can pray for wisdom to make the best decision possible. You also can, and should, keep your eyes and ears open for problems, and be ready to do what it takes to solve them. But you can't protect your precious, vulnerable little "Dumbo" from every hurt and failure.

Because you're trusting Christ, your child is heir to all God's promises to you, even if he is too young in mind or body to look to Him on his own. And one of God's promises is that He never wastes the hurts we have to suffer, but uses them to make us the people He created us to be. Look to Him in faith, dear parent, and then do your homework and step out, doing the best you know. He will bless you and your child as you do so.

CHAPTER 5

Stims, Rituals, and OBSESSIONS

"I realize how far we have come."

MY MOTHER'S FAVORITE picture of Eric was taken when he was about eight. She says she loves that picture because his face full of freckles reminds her of Tom Sawyer. It is an adorable picture, but I have mixed feelings about it. You see, the year Eric was four, he picked little bits of skin off of his face in hundreds of places. Where he picked, the skin bled, and then formed a scab. When the scabs fell off, the healing areas were especially sensitive to the sun. Every place that once had a scab soon developed a freckle. Even though Eric hadn't picked at his skin for years by that time, his freckles were unusually noticeable in this picture, because it was taken during the summer when the sun brought them out.

It is unspeakably painful to watch your precious child injure himself! When I look at Eric's "freckle picture," I remember the desperate grief and helplessness I felt about Eric's scab-covered little face, and how I cried out to God to show me how to make him stop hurting himself. But I also have other emotions. The picture fills me with joy as I realize how far we have come. I thank God for His incredible mercies in our lives! In this chapter, I'm going to share what I learned about modifying stims and rituals, and keeping obsessions under control.

WHAT ARE STIMS AND OTHER RELATED HABITS?

Eric's habit of pulling skin off of his face is what experts call a self-stimulation, or "stim" for short. Most autism spectrum kids stim at some point in their development, and while many never injure themselves like Eric did, some do. This drive to self-stimulate is seen not only in autism spectrum kids, but also in developmentally challenged kids with a variety of other diagnoses, and those who have sustained severe head trauma. So this habit tendency develops because of brain differences.

Stims seem to help spectrum kids feel better. They stim when they are anxious, frustrated, or bored. And for whatever reason, stimming is very gratifying. Even when it is painful, it's a difficult habit to break. But stimming interferes with learning, because when a spectrum kid is stimming, he's paying attention to his stim, not to what you are trying to teach him. Stims also set a child apart from his typical peers because they mark him as different. So it is important to find ways to help your child break this habit.

Do you remember when I mentioned rituals and obsessions in chapter 2? Many experts classify these behaviors as more complex stims. They tend to be driven by the same kinds of feelings as stims, and they also seem to help spectrum kids cope. But like stims, rituals and obsessions can interfere with normal life. Whether your child flaps his hands at the wrist and spins in a circle constantly, asks you hundreds of times a day whether it's dark outside (in the daytime!), melts down if he's not home to watch his favorite TV program at the same time every day, or checks to be sure that each clock in the house is accurate numerous times a day, stims and related habits have the potential to completely run your child's life (and yours).

TYPICAL PEOPLE HAVE HABITS, TOO

Do you stim? I'm sure you'd say that you don't. But consider: Do you rub your chin when you're thinking hard? Absentmindedly twirl a lock of hair around your finger? Drum your fingers on a tabletop when you're bored?

Habits can comfort us when we're under stress, distract us when we're bored, and give organization and structure to our lives.

How about rituals? Do you put on your left shoe first every day, then your right? Do you find repetitive actions, like folding laundry or washing dishes, oddly comforting or relaxing?

What's the difference between an obsession and a strong interest? Do you have hobbies? Buy books by your favorite author as soon as they come out? Collect stamps or antiques?

Habits can comfort us when we're under stress, distract us when we're bored, and give organization and structure to our lives. Our special interests give us joy and enrich our leisure time. Some of us are even fortunate enough to be able to make a living pursuing their interests, as I do.

The difference between you and your spectrum child is that your habits and interests don't interfere with your daily life, and you don't focus all your attention on them. You can watch TV, talk to your child, and fold laundry at the same time. You can twirl that lock of hair and drive your car at the same time. You're also able to limit these habits when you need to. If you have an odd or embarrassing habit, you probably practice it only in private. And you don't let your interests run your life. If you're interested in clocks, you may read books about clock making, or collect timepieces. But you probably don't draw clocks compulsively, tell everyone you meet about Greenwich Mean Time, or stop strangers on the street and ask them to let you look at their watches. If you get carried away about your interest and begin to bore someone, you notice his lack of enthusiasm and stop talking.

Understanding that the difference between your habits and your child's have to do with their appropriateness, scope, and tenacity can enable you to craft responses that aim to not eliminate them, but to modify them. Your child is about as likely to completely stop stimming and developing routines and interests as you are. Since routines and interests are natural human tendencies, your goal is to help your child move from being controlled (and controlling others) by his habits to bringing them under control.

DEALING WITH STIMS

Eric wasn't allowed to stim during his ABA drills, because they interfered with his attention. Every time he began, he was given the instruction "Hands quiet," and the behaviorist moved Eric's hands to the table, if necessary. Over time, the habit weakened because he had fewer opportunities to practice it. At the same time, he was mastering more complex skills, and he began to find those more interesting.

For example, when his ABA treatment began, Eric couldn't stack one block on top of another one to build a tower. Left to himself, he lined them up, end to end, in a single line along the floor. There was no creativity and no purpose to this repetitive activity. But his behaviorist taught block-building behavior one small step at a time. Eventually, Eric could build block towers on command. Then he began building block towers on his own, during his free playtime. Technically speaking, he was still stimulating himself, in that he was performing a repetitive activity, but rather than disfiguring himself by picking at his skin, or lining up blocks in the same way, he was doing what we call "playing." This kind of progression demonstrates your goal as you work with your child's stims. Since totally eliminating them is impossible, you want to encourage them to develop into more typical and enjoyable behaviors.

If your child can participate in an ABA-based early intervention program, his stimming will naturally decrease as he acquires more complex skills. But if he's past the age for early intervention and still stims, this doesn't mean that there are no solutions for him. You can still limit his opportunities to stim, as Eric's behaviorist did, and you can also replace meaningless repetitive activity with more meaningful activity by teaching him new play skills.

LIMITING OPPORTUNITIES TO STIM

How do you go about limiting your child's ability to stim? Behaviorists recommend a variety of techniques. First and most obvious, you can physically stop him by taking his hand away or telling him to stop. I started out doing what the behaviorist did, except instead of saying, "Hands quiet," I took advantage of Eric's attraction to music by singing, "No picking" in a high-pitched, rising tone. At first I had to take his hand away from his face as I gave the instruction. But in time I could just sing the instruction in a teasing voice, and he'd respond with, "Yes picking!" with the same tone and teasing voice, and take his hand away himself.

Another way to limit opportunities to stim is to require your child to go a certain number of minutes without stimming before being allowed to do it again. For example, you might say, "You may not wiggle your fingers until you've folded two towels." Once the towels are folded, he can do his stim for a brief period, and then fold two more towels. You can use any task, requiring him to give his full attention and effort to it for a prescribed period. Homework is a great one to choose, since if he's stimming while he is supposed to be doing schoolwork, he's not giving it his undivided attention. His learning will improve as his ability to stim is restricted. Over time you can increase the amount of time required to "earn" access to stimming, and decrease the amount of time you'll allow him to stim. Over time, this may weaken his habit.

Another limiting technique involves restricting access to the stim to certain times of day or locations. If your child has odd stims that draw attention when he's in public, you can tell him that he may do his stim only *after* you leave the grocery store. You can make the dinner table a "stim-free zone." Or you can tell him that he can only stim in his room or, better, only in a room he doesn't like to be in. Over time you can increase the places where stims are forbidden, and decrease the time spent in the places where they are permitted. This should also weaken the habit.

TEACHING NEW PLAY SKILLS

In addition to limiting access to stims, you'll want to teach your child new ways to occupy himself. As you discover which play skills he especially likes, you'll notice that he's drawn to play that captures the essence of what he enjoys about the stim. So he may not want to play "cops and robbers" with you, but he'll probably be attracted to quiet, repetitive play. A child who likes to line up blocks or cars in a row might enjoy lining up the cars of a toy train that has magnetic connectors, for example.

Eric liked to line things up, so I got him a starter wooden train set—just an engine and two cars with magnetic connectors, and enough track to make a one-foot diameter circle. It took some effort to get him to put the train on the track and push it back and forth, but once he was enjoying doing this I showed him how to push the train around the circular track. When he started doing this on his own, I added a piece that converted the simple circle into a figure-eight track and showed him how to push the train across the connector. As time went on I built more and more complex track configurations, with bridges and tunnels, and showed him all the possibilities by pushing the train around each new creation myself until he imitated it. And I changed the configuration frequently so he wouldn't get fixated on one setup.

Eric loved the story of *The Little Engine That Could*.[1] One day I was thrilled to enter his room and discover that he'd built a "mountain" out of Play-Doh and run a wooden track up one side of it and down the other. He had his toy train on the track and was pushing it up his mountain, chanting to himself, "I think I can, I think I can." Eric had gone from meaningless, repetitive action (lining things up), to not only playing, but also playing *creatively*. Later, he began building his own track configurations, just like any other kid his age. How exciting it was to see him go from self-stimulation to creative play!

DEALING WITH ROUTINES

As I mentioned, all people develop routines. Routines are complex habits that help us organize ourselves, and their monotony may soothe us during times of stress. The problem with autism spectrum routines is that they tend to control the spectrum kid and his loved ones. Common routines include insisting on wearing the same clothes every day, melting down unless the same route is taken to school every day, or insisting on being home to watch a favorite TV show every day.

Because spectrum routines become rigid and controlling, I was constantly on the watch for evidence that Eric was developing new ones. I wanted to be able to nip disruptive routines in the bud before they became settled habits. Where disruptive routines were already in place, I worked to modify them. An example of how I did this is the way I taught Eric not to pull Coco's tail, told in chapter 3.

But preventing and modifying disruptive routines is only half the story. Since it is natural for people to develop routines, helping your child develop routines that are functional rather than disruptive will give her the ability to organize and structure her life in a more useful way. Just as you may feel calmer in the midst of a crisis if you engage in a mindless, repetitive task, your child will feel better when she's under stress if she has tasks that she can use to distract herself. If she learns routines that serve the same purpose as yours do, which is to make life simpler, she'll feel better. This greater sense of self-control will probably result in her having somewhat less of a tendency to try to control her environment (and you).

So besides trying to prevent Eric from developing disruptive routines, I taught him valuable routines and life skills. For example, I taught him to dress himself in the same way every day. If you don't teach this to your child in an organized, stepwise fashion, he may come out of his room wearing his underpants on *top* of his trousers! So I went from dressing Eric silently to speaking each step to him. "First we take off our pajamas. Then we put on our underpants. . . ." As I did this, Eric began to see the order in what I was doing instead of passively submitting to it without paying attention. Next I told him what to do, one step at a time, and waited for him to do each step. I also needed to teach buttons and zippers separately before he was able to do these on command. Then I faded my assistance by only giving instructions if he stopped paying attention to what he was doing or forgot the next step. Finally I was able to say, "Get dressed," and Eric could do it all by himself.

Any skill can be taught in this way. When Eric was older I taught him to make his bed, sweep the floor, clean the bathroom, fold laundry, and do his own wash in the same stepwise fashion. The more functional routines he could do on his own, the less attracted he was to creating his own meaningless routines. These had the same organizing and self-soothing qualities as his made-up routines, but also offered the added pleasure of having done a *real* job well. And I always made sure to praise him lavishly for his increasing ability to help at home.

DEALING WITH OBSESSIONS

Generally speaking, kids with lower function tend to focus on stims and slavish devotion to routine, while kids with higher function will be more likely to develop obsessions. Dr. Tony Attwood, a world-renowned expert on Asperger syndrome, prefers the term "special interests" to "obsessions."[2] This is a gracious and accepting way to describe the phenomenon, but it is also fair to say that some people with Asperger syndrome become obsessed with their special interest. So I'm choosing to use the word *obsession* here to emphasize that our goal is to help our children modify their obsessions so that they can become true "special interests."

These interests are not only enjoyable for your child in the short term, but they also can provide common ground for relationships, which are ultimately a richer source of gratification for adults. But unfortunately, many higher-functioning people with Asperger syndrome tend to bore or alienate others, because they share their interest with those who are indifferent to it, or they lecture instead of conversing.

Bill Bryson, a humor writer, tells a funny, yet heartbreaking tale of sharing a train car with a "train spotter," a man with Asperger syndrome who is obsessed with the mechanical details about trains and the schedules on which they run.[3] In this story, Bryson admits to feeling sorry for the man, but he also expresses his deep irritation over being trapped with a bore. If you're the parent of an Aspie, you may be able to empathize with his irritation. It may seem easier in the short run to let your child rattle on, and especially because you want him to feel good about himself. But in the long run, you'll be doing your child a favor if you help him to modify his obsession into a special interest and learn to interact more considerately with others about it.

"NEW RUSSIA"

Eric's longest-running obsession was an imaginary country, which he created when he was eight years old. New Russia was born when Eric noticed that a peninsula on the east coast of Russia bore a superficial similarity to the peninsula where our home city was located. We were studying geography and the adventurers who explored the New World at the time. That afternoon Eric "discovered" a sand dune on the beach near our house and named it New Russia.

> *It would have been easy just to listen to him talk, but instead I dialogued with him.*

Eric talked constantly about New Russia! He decreed its political structure and foreign policy. He experimented with creating a New Russian language, and with writing a constitution. He progressively annexed more and more of the beach, and when I commented that there were no citizens of New Russia, he began annexing our neighborhood, as well. He drew borders on the sidewalk with chalk. He drew maps of New Russia. He even created New Russian recipes!

It was clear that Eric saw himself as the undisputed potentate of his fantasy country. This provided a way for Eric to feel in control, important, and powerful. It would have been easy just to listen to him talk, but knowing that obsessions like this continue to grow, and resist change more and more as time goes on, instead I dialogued with him about it. I reminded him that citizens decide for themselves what their form of government is, and who their leaders are. I constantly referred to New Russia as a "game," and urged him to "play" it with other kids.

One day Eric did share his fantasy world. "I'm the president of New Russia," Eric confided to his friend.

"Yeah, well, I'm the *king* of New Russia!" David retorted. And so began a mutual negotiation in real life that deprived Eric's fantasy of its solitary, obsessive appeal. Over time, it became a shared activity. Later, Eric moved on to other interests that incorporated elements of New Russia but were more reality-based. After New Russia, Eric wrote fantasy stories about foreign lands instead of setting up physical borders in an actual geographic location.

FROM OBSESSION TO SPECIAL INTEREST

Your child may be obsessed with collecting stopwatches, or with reciting facts about outer space. But if you can find ways to connect these solitary, repetitive activities to a real pursuit, or introduce social elements, you may find the interest will change. For example, I might try to turn an obsession with collecting stopwatches into an interest in using a stopwatch to time events. Once the child was excited about timing things, I'd try to interest her in sprinting by timing her with the stopwatch while she ran, and then urge her to improve her time. As the interest became less about stopwatches and more about running, it might even be possible to interest her in joining a track team, thus incorporating social elements in the interest. The spectrum kid who likes to recite facts might be persuaded to participate in spelling bees, math Olympiads, or trivia contests. This would introduce a more adaptive social element into what is, otherwise, just verbal stimming in the presence of observers. And if she's the best at her special interest, she might even win a measure of fame for her ability!

Every parent can find ways to minimize the negative impact of obsessive special interests by thinking creatively about how to modify them.

Eventually, a self-stimulatory interest may even develop into a skill that others will pay your child to perform. Think of it—ballerinas are women who obsessively refine their skill in toe walking and twirling, which are repetitive movements that many spectrum kids perform when they are small! Scientists are people who have transmuted their fascination over some natural phenomena into study of a discipline to which they can contribute new, creative insights. A wag once commented that the whole Silicon Valley is just one big sheltered workshop for Aspies with computer interests!

Eric channeled his early interest in foreign countries, cultures, and languages into a love for language learning and travel. It didn't just happen, but with much direction and encouragement, it did happen. Depending on your child's level of function, this may or may not be possible for him. But every parent can find ways to minimize the negative impact of obsessive special interests by thinking creatively about how to modify them.

GETTING TO THE HEART

It's important to reach your child's heart rather than settling for simply modifying his behavior, as you help him move from stims to productive activities. An important behavioral principle is that motivation matters. I learned from Eric's behaviorist how to analyze his behavior to learn why he did what he did. This was important, because once I understood why Eric engaged in a behavior, I often could find a replacement that captured the gratification it offered, without the negative results.

The Bible also teaches that the way we behave springs from the motives of our hearts. For example, Jesus said that what we speak originates in our hearts (Luke 6:45), and that our behavior springs from our thoughts, and results in our actions (Matthew 15:19). And so as your higher-functioning child gets older, you'll want to begin to help him understand what moves him to do what he does, and teach him to respond to the motives of his heart more appropriately or righteously. This can mean helping him to find a way to replace a socially unacceptable stim with something more neutral, or make his own choice to engage in it only in private. It can also mean helping him see that he does some things because he's anxious, and that when he is anxious, controlling others makes him feel safer.

The problem is, when he chooses a behavior that's motivated by a heart's desire to control those around him so he can feel safer, he's sacrificing others' interests to serve his own. But Jesus taught that his goal should be to serve others ahead of himself (Mark 10:42–45). The apostle Paul tells us in Galatians 5:23 that the fruit of the Spirit is self-control. This is contrasted with the works of the flesh (Galatians 5:20), which include things like strife and fits of anger—the very things your child may do to enable him to continue engaging in his stim, ritual, or obsession. And so as he grows in faith, you'll want to teach him to recognize when he's anxious or angry, and consciously choose behaviors that are less self-centered. I'll be addressing this subject in more detail in the next chapter, which deals with managing emotions.

CHAPTER 6

Managing
EMOTIONS

"We still had a lot to learn about his emotions."

I THINK THAT MOST autism spectrum parents would agree that meltdowns are one of the biggest challenges that they face. This was certainly how I felt! When Eric was three, he melted down every time I tried to introduce any change in his life, and was only happy when he was sitting quietly and stimming. If I placed any demands upon him, he became anxious and melted down. But over time, early intervention training and the principles I've discussed in chapters 2 through 5 helped him to become comfortable engaging in a much broader range of activities.

By the time Eric was about six, the meltdowns had pretty much disappeared. What's more, he'd become an unusually cooperative, obedient, and eager-to-please little boy. Envious parents of typical children who didn't know his history often asked me for the secret of my parenting success. This was certainly a new experience for me!

Looking back on those peaceful years, I've become convinced that Eric was so easy to handle because I was his emotional anchor. He looked to me to organize his life, relied upon me to show him how to respond to unpredictable circumstances, and trusted me completely. He wasn't without anxiety in those years, but because he knew that I'd help him cope with whatever happened, he wasn't overwhelmed by it. We even traveled in Europe together twice as a family during those years, staying in a new hotel every day or two, and Eric handled the transitions beautifully.

While typical kids also go through a period of innocent faith in their parents, it generally doesn't last as long as Eric's did, and their trust usually isn't as complete. So Eric's extreme compliance was not standard for spectrum kids. His complete trust, no less than the earlier meltdowns, was a consequence of his autism spectrum differences.

Then came adolescence. Some days it seemed as though space aliens must have stolen my sweet boy and replaced him with an evil clone! As Eric became a preteen, he began to realize that I wasn't an all-knowing font of wisdom. As he increasingly recognized my fallibility, he began to feel less safe entrusting himself to me, and wanted to manage his own affairs by himself. There's nothing unusual about a child developing insights and desires like these in adolescence. The problem was that Eric's remaining spectrum challenges made it more difficult for him to manage on his own. Anxiety again began to overwhelm him, and he reacted as he had when he was a preschooler, with meltdowns.

> *Our autism spectrum kids experience the same anxieties we all do, only far, far more intensely.*

It was a good thing, and a sign of real growth, that Eric learned that he couldn't place his full, unconditional faith and trust in me. This happens in typical kids, and it needed to happen for Eric, too. To become a man, he had to learn to look in faith to God, not to me, and manage his own life. But the transition was confusing for all of us because the changes in Eric were so abrupt and dramatic.

MOST SPECTRUM KIDS
STRUGGLE WITH THEIR EMOTIONS

Most spectrum kids, both high and low functioning, experience severe turmoil as they make the transition from childhood to adolescence. But if you can recognize what emotions motivate your child's behavior, you may be able to help him learn to handle his emotions and achieve greater independence during his teen years. It took a lot of work before Eric and I began to understand the feelings that drove his behavior, and discovered how to manage them better. This chapter will help you do this with your child. I'll start with a general discussion of the kinds of emotions that produce disturbing behaviors. Then I'll explain some biblical principles that govern our emotional life, and suggest practical tips for helping your child stay in control of himself.

THE THREE MAIN EMOTIONS
THAT MOTIVATE PROBLEM BEHAVIORS

I'm sure you've noticed already that when your child is emotionally overwhelmed, he tends to melt down or isolate. Let's consider the three main emotions that tend to produce these behaviors.

Anxiety

Our autism spectrum kids experience the same anxieties we all do, only far, far more intensely. Because of sensory differences, your child may find even ordinary experiences overpowering. His communication challenges make understanding what's going on around him more difficult, and he's much slower in his mental processing. This means he recognizes and responds to change much more slowly than you do. He also has difficulty realizing that he's becoming disturbed, determining what's bothering him, and articulating it to others.

Doctors will tell you that the two basic responses to an anxiety-provoking situation are "fight" and "flight." Typical people employ an infinite number of different, subtle variations on the basic "fight or flight" theme when they face stressful situations. For example, sarcasm may be used to express hostility more subtly, while changing the subject is a way to escape an unwanted conversation. But for spectrum people, under pressure and already overwhelmed emotionally, it can be just about impossible to come up with a creative response. They tend to employ two very basic responses: melting down, or withdrawing from the situation that troubles them. So when your spectrum child melts down or "zones out," you can be pretty sure he's feeling overwhelmed.

Depression

Depression is more common in higher-functioning kids, because people expect more of them. A lower-functioning kid has fewer social interests, and fewer demands are made of him. He also has less awareness of, and concern for, the opinions of others. But an Asperger kid in a mainstream school program may feel like a failure all day long. He's probably slow and uncoordinated in PE class, and he may struggle with academics, too. Even if he's very bright, processing difficulties may slow his performance. He almost certainly will experience some rejection, and maybe even mistreatment, from his typical peers. Because coping with the demands of a constantly changing environment is hard work, he may find himself continually feeling mentally exhausted.

Because spectrum kids aren't good at labeling and understanding their feelings, they tend to respond to sad feelings in much the same way as they react to anxious feelings—that's right, by melting down or isolating. Feelings of depression can overwhelm them suddenly, and while in the grip of a meltdown they may be at risk for harming themselves impulsively or striking out at others. This kind of overwhelmed sadness can pass as quickly as it appears, though, so you may be amazed to find your thirteen-year-old, who just said that he wanted to die, playing video games as if he didn't have a care in the world. Your child may also choose to respond to sad feelings with anger because, for many, it's easier to be mad than sad. Dr. Tony Attwood quotes an Asperger syndrome teen as saying, "Crying doesn't work, so I get angry instead and throw sticks."[1]

Anger

It's easy to see how anger leads to meltdowns. Your child may use anger as a kind of all-purpose emotion. A meltdown can drive away those whose presence disturbs him, or pressure you to remove him from a confusing environment. Some kids use anger as a self-protective device, to keep those they fear away from them. It can also help them achieve dominance over other kids on the playground by making them afraid. Melting down makes others more willing to adapt to them, so they don't have to change. Many spectrum kids find that they feel unusually calm after a meltdown, so they may learn to use anger as a tension reliever. It should go without saying that, while this reduces your child's tension, it puts yours through the roof!

Typical kids also use anger in some of these ways when they're young, but as they grow they develop more mature coping skills and better self-control. It takes spectrum kids much longer to learn these lessons, because their anxiety and processing slowness work against them. I'm sure that you don't learn things well when you're anxious, either. So your child will need your frequent, consistent, patient biblical rebuke and correction, along with lots of concrete suggestions for other ways to solve his problems.

FOR LOWER-FUNCTIONING KIDS

You may find that your lower-functioning child will continue to need you to structure his environment and prevent meltdowns indefinitely. But I wouldn't just decide that my child's function is too low for him to learn to manage himself, if I were you. You might be surprised at what he can learn if you're patient and willing to keep repeating yourself indefinitely. Remember the tortoise and the hare!

SPECTRUM ANGER IS DIFFERENT

It's important to understand that autism spectrum anger is different than typical anger. When you get angry, there are gradations in your response. You might be a little miffed, pretty irritated, or absolutely enraged, depending on the circumstance. But your spectrum child can come completely unglued without even realizing it, until he's totally out of control, and it can happen almost instantaneously. Dr. Attwood says that it's as though spectrum people have only an on-off switch for their anger, while typical people have something more like a dimmer switch, enabling them to advance through subtle gradations of feeling.[2] You may be perplexed because you have no idea how your child became so angry, so quickly. And once he is in this kind of blind rage, he probably will be unable to back down until he first calms down. In the meantime, the more he expresses his anger, the more infuriated he becomes.

MELTDOWN TRIGGERS

Although meltdowns often appear spontaneous at first glance, if you study your child you'll begin to recognize what triggers them. Common triggers for most kids include anything that might provoke anxiety, like change, noise, or sensory overload. Your child may also become angry if he thinks you are angry. And because spectrum kids aren't good at reading the emotions of others from their facial expression and tone of voice, speaking to him in a loud voice may be enough for him to draw this conclusion.

Any kind of expression of strong emotion, even love and concern, can provoke an angry response in some spectrum kids.

She may also melt down if she's confronted too strongly. This is why speaking "low and slow," as I discussed in chapter 3, is so essential. And if what you have to say is likely to provoke strong emotions in her, she may cope better if you don't look her straight in the eye as you say it. I've found that difficult conversations go better if they're discussed while driving in the car, because I have to keep my eyes on the road. Autism behavior specialist Carol Gray recommends a side-by-side posture to discuss difficult material, while drawing pictures, to help your younger or lower-functioning child visualize what you're trying to tell her.[3]

Any kind of expression of strong emotion, even love and concern, can provoke an angry response in some spectrum kids. They seem to find the emotional content overwhelming. Perhaps it's just too much to handle at a time when they're already stressed out just trying to understand what's happening. Adding strong emotion puts many of them over the top. Some kids will also melt down if they are physically restrained. Even hugs can do this. So can asking, "What's the matter?" This is because if something is already bothering them and they aren't sure what it is, being asked to explain may be the straw that breaks the camel's back.

PREVENTING MELTDOWNS

You'll notice that everything I'm telling you can trigger a meltdown in a spectrum child is something you would naturally do with a typical child who's beginning to get upset. This means that you'll need to retrain your natural responses if you're going to be able to help your child calm down.

For me, the hardest part was coping with my own feelings. If I wasn't treating Eric as I'd like to be treated, I felt as if I wasn't treating him lovingly. Remembering to behave in a manner that feels "wrong" is a constant struggle, and sometimes even after all these years, I still forget. And this makes sense, doesn't it? Christ defined loving others as treating them the way you want to be treated (Matthew 7:12; 22:39, 40).

The challenge here is to remember that your child is different. To show love to him, you need to treat him the way you would like to be treated *if you were on the autism spectrum*. Don't be discouraged if, even after learning this, you still find it difficult to speak in a quiet monotone, without much eye contact. Just keep trying; you'll get better at it in time.

PRACTICAL HELPS THAT MAY REDUCE TENSION

Other interventions that may help prevent meltdowns are regular physical exercise and relaxation activities. When Eric came home from school obviously jangled, sending him out to run around the block often helped, as did letting him go to his room and spend some quiet time alone. As he got older, he began enjoying walking with me, which enabled us to have those "no eye contact" conversations I mentioned earlier. Since people who are conversing while they walk don't look at each other much, it's a great opportunity to connect emotionally while you're helping your child calm down.

Some kids find engaging in their special interest calming. Others are relaxed by engaging in repetitive activities. A lower-functioning kid might rock back and forth, or line toys up. If you've taught your child to enjoy *purposeful* repetitive activity, as I mentioned in chapter 5, you may even be blessed to find that sweeping the floor for you is just what he needs to help him settle down!

WHAT ABOUT MEDICATIONS?

Some parents have found that medicines help their less able kids, who don't profit as much from some of the relaxation and communication techniques I've just mentioned. These keep their child in a less tense state, so it takes more stress to upset them. The result may be fewer meltdowns. But because these medicines can have serious side effects, I recommend that parents exhaust all other possibilities before trying them.[4]

Many graduates of ABA early intervention programs seem to move "up the spectrum" in their behavior and ability. This is surely the best way to avoid problems that can be associated with medicine use. But it isn't always possible, particularly with older or less able kids. For these kids, medicine is a blessing that enables them to remain at home and stay engaged in school and community life.

HOW TO RESOLVE A MELTDOWN

Once your child is in a meltdown, it's crucial to know how to respond in a way that helps him pull out of it. Meltdowns can become self-perpetuating, particularly if the problem that prompted the meltdown isn't promptly addressed, and they can literally last for hours. So it's important to defuse the situation as soon as possible.

Once again, you'll find that most of your instinctive responses to meltdowns will tend to increase their severity. Any attempt to touch or hug may even provoke physical violence while your child is in this heightened emotional state. Any strong emotion you express will increase his anger and anxiety. On the other hand, speaking in a very quiet, calm, in-control voice will make him feel safer. If you express fear or confusion, this will frighten him and make him feel unsafe, because he's probably counting on your maintaining control of the situation. So project quiet confidence as you talk to him.

There's no point in arguing or trying to explain anything to her while she's in this state. Emotionally speaking, she is blinded by her anxiety and anger, and won't be able to process what you say. Arguing with her will make it much worse—particularly if *you* become angry at what appears to be a refusal to listen. I had to learn this the hard way!

Sending your child to his room or to a quiet place will help him calm down. Leave him completely alone, if possible. If he's higher functioning, allowing him to distract himself with a favorite solitary activity may help. But less able kids in this state are agitated by any unnecessary stimulation, so they should be left alone in a quiet, safe environment with nothing in it that might distract them.

THE ROLE OF DISCIPLINE IN MELTDOWNS

Once the meltdown is over, you might be tempted to just be grateful that your child has calmed down, and pretend it never happened for fear of provoking him again. But God's Word commands us to correct our child's behavior. As we discovered in chapter 3, God hasn't granted an exemption from discipline to special-needs kids. But the way we *apply* this biblical principle must take into account our kids' differences if our discipline is to be effective.

If you spank a typical child who is "pitching a fit," this will probably calm him down, once he's finished crying. But spanking your spectrum child during a meltdown will make it much worse. It produces painful physical contact, and your attempts at correction will not be understood while he is emotionally out of control. This doesn't mean that you shouldn't spank your spectrum child if he behaved sinfully during his meltdown. But it does mean that you should wait until he's calmed down, so that he's able to think clearly about what he's done wrong, repent, and pray for grace to resist temptation the next time.

DOING WHAT COMES NATURALLY

Unfortunately, not having the benefit of this advice when Eric began melting down again as a preteen, I did what came naturally. He'd been so cooperative for so long, and there was so little evidence of any remaining spectrum issues, that I didn't realize that we still had a lot to learn about his emotions. I really thought that Eric had become no different than any typical kid I knew. And in some ways, I was right. But in other ways, our hardest work was still ahead of us.

> *We have to address what's going on in our child's heart, which is the source of his motivation and decision making.*

And so when I tell you that I did what came naturally, I'm telling you that I spoke heatedly to him. Sometimes I cried. I tried to touch and hug him. I entreated him, speaking of my love for him. All of these genuine expressions of a loving mother's heart made Eric *more* angry and out of control. Finally, my wise pastor suggested leaving him alone to calm down for a while, and returning to biblical correction once he was calm.

I hit the books and learned that this kind of emotional difficulty in adolescence is very common in people with spectrum issues, and discovered some of the things that I'm now teaching you. Even more important, I sought the Lord diligently for wisdom on how to apply the principles of biblical discipline to this challenging situation. God answered that prayer, and I learned how to help Eric in a manner that's consistent with his differences, but is also consistent with biblical truth. Today he's better at recognizing when he needs to calm down, and taking the necessary actions for himself.

ARE MELTDOWNS SINFUL?

We've spent a lot of time addressing practical issues related to meltdowns, which could cause you to conclude that they're just behaviors that we need to prevent. But because the Bible has so much to say on the subject of sinful anger, we can't just stay at the level of behavior. We have to address what's going on in our child's heart, which is the source of his motivation and decision making. Does a spectrum child have a physical issue that makes him prone to experiencing uncontrolled emotions? I have no doubt whatsoever that this is the case. But does this mean that when he melts down, it's not his fault? That's not what Scripture teaches.

The Bible is full of admonitions against sinful anger. We are commanded to put off angry behaviors of all kinds, and replace them with kindness and self-control (Colossians 3:8–14). Nowhere in Scripture is there any suggestion that our behavior is not our fault. Rather, the Bible consistently teaches that we express through our behavior what is already inside of our hearts (Matthew 15:19). We've already looked at some of the reasons why your child might melt down. And while you can understand and have great compassion for his struggles, it's your responsibility as a parent to help him find other ways to deal with his emotions. Meltdowns are sinful, and we need to help our children replace them with godly behaviors.

AFTER IT'S OVER

Once your child has calmed down, it's time to talk to him about what he's done wrong and discipline him in a manner appropriate to his level of understanding. This will probably include spanking if he's younger or lower functioning. But, especially for older and higher-functioning kids, the biblical correction you'll offer will be far more important than the consequences you impose. Because your child has a physical challenge that predisposes him to the sin of uncontrolled anger, you can expect that this is a tendency he'll find difficult to conquer. Helping him understand what's going on inside of him, to the extent he is capable of it, will be crucial to his mastering it.

ERIC'S WAY

Eric had gotten too big to spank. Because he needed all the social experience he could get, grounding him worked against his best interests, although I did try it for a while. I also restricted television and video games, and added extra chores, but I found that consequences weren't having the desired effect on him. It seemed that when he was anxious he'd pass a "point of no return," emotionally speaking, and once this happened a meltdown was inevitable. And trying to avoid being grounded before a big event made him very anxious. It was a vicious cycle!

I was trying to be consistent, so I imposed consequences for each episode of unacceptable behavior. But because the meltdowns were happening so frequently, the penalties mounted quickly and were having an embittering, rather than a motivating, effect on Eric. We had to find another way.

I took a two-pronged approach. First, when I recognized that his tension was rising, I'd take some of the actions I recommended in the prevention section of this chapter. But I also wanted him to be able to recognize the signs that his tension was rising for himself, rather than always depending upon me to help him stay calm. So after a meltdown, I'd ask him, "What could you have done instead?" and we'd discuss alternatives to the course of behavior he'd chosen that had led to the meltdown.

> *I can honestly say that I learned as much about myself as I did about my son's challenges.*

Since the threat of consequences wasn't motivating Eric, and it seemed that he had less ability to control himself after he'd passed a certain point, it was crucial for him to learn to recognize his anger as early as possible, and take steps to calm himself down before he reached that point. We began to work on recognizing the warning signs of a meltdown by talking about what was happening inside of him just before he lost control. Eventually he learned to recognize the changes in himself.

We also studied what God's Word says about uncontrolled anger. It seemed to me that recognizing the *sinfulness* of his sin was crucial to motivate him to give up what had become a habitual response to the tension he felt. So we read through the book of Proverbs, looking for principles to explain his angry responses.[5] We also read books on anger.[6] Eric began counseling with an elder from our church, to whom he could confide struggles he was experiencing with his feelings toward *me*.

As time went on, I began to recognize the role I was playing in provoking Eric to anger. This included my own sinful choices, as well as my emotional style of communication. Isn't that just the way God works in our lives? We start out trying to help our child deal with a besetting sin, and end up discovering our own. I can honestly say that I learned as much about myself, and my own sinful patterns, as I did about my son's challenges and sinful choices during those years.

The turning point came when Eric recognized that melting down should not even be an option, because God forbids unrestrained expressions of anger. Because God has saved us by the blood of His Son, the only appropriate response is gratitude for His goodness, and obedience to His commands through the power the Holy Spirit gives us to live a holy life (Romans 12:1–2). This doesn't mean that Eric has completely stopped responding in sinful anger, but now he's fighting the good fight of faith and looking to God for the power to do His will. I wish I could give you a five-step method for producing this realization in your child, but it's something that only God can do in his heart.

FOR LOWER-FUNCTIONING TEENS

It's important to recognize that some spectrum kids may not achieve a level of function that will make it possible to develop self-control without ongoing help from you. If your child is lower functioning, she may continue to need your help to recognize and prevent impending meltdowns. But self-control, rather than being controlled by you, is always a desirable goal, if it's achievable for your child.

Regardless of her level of function, you'll find that self-control probably won't develop in your spectrum child as quickly as it does for your typical kids. You may be tempted to be discouraged by her lack of progress. Here it's essential to heed Scripture's admonition: "Let us not grow weary of doing good, for in due season we will reap, if we do not give up" (Galatians 6:9). God has commanded us to bring up our children in the discipline and instruction of the Lord (Ephesians 6:4). He hasn't commanded us to be successful parents; He's commanded us to be *faithful* parents.

Our loving heavenly Father knows our kids far better than we ever will. He knows what your child is capable of, and what he's not. As you look for opportunities to help him grow in self-control, God will give you the grace to be patient and gentle with him, even if his progress seems disappointing. As you seek to be faithful, bring your concerns to God in prayer, and leave the results to Him, He'll provide.

CHAPTER 7

The
RELATIONSHIP PUZZLE

"God promises enough grace to meet any
need His people may have."

AS A SMALL BOY with autism, Eric didn't seem to notice other kids at
all. He wasn't included, but didn't seem to care, either. It hurt me to know that
he was different, but he didn't seem to have any awareness of it, and wasn't disturbed by it.

As I've mentioned, autistic children sometimes "move up the spectrum" after
a successful early intervention. This happened with Eric, and by the time he was
school age, he *was* interested in other kids. By the time he was a teen, he was very
interested, but the interest wasn't always reciprocated. Those were painful years
for Eric. I told him repeatedly that high school was probably the last setting he
would ever be where "cool" was everything. I assured him that in college he'd
find people who'd be interested in the things that interested him, rather than
being chiefly concerned with how well he fit in.

Eric began university as a commuter student. I'll never forget the first time
that he called to let me know that he wouldn't be home for dinner, because he
had plans of his own with a classmate. Oh, the joy! Since then, calls like this
have come regularly. At the end of his freshman year, Eric told me, "Mom, you
were right about how college would be different from high school." He hasn't

become Mr. Popularity, but he now has a satisfying social life.

This can happen for your child, too, but I wouldn't be honest if I didn't make it clear that this won't be an easy transition for either of you to make. It's also painfully true that not every spectrum adult will achieve the level of intimacy he longs for in a friendship. But any child's natural social abilities can be improved, especially if he recognizes his need and is motivated to change.

> *A spectrum kid may tend to avoid his peers,*
> *finding it easier to interact with adults.*

This chapter will begin by describing the spectrum differences that make social interaction a challenge. Then I'll offer suggestions on how to help your child deal with peer difficulties and develop the social skills he needs to build satisfying relationships. Finally, I'll discuss how to nurture the most important relationship your child will ever have—with God.

CONTROL

Spectrum kids are not as naturally interested in people as typical kids are. Generally speaking, they prefer objects and facts to people and relationships. As a young child, Eric was attracted to objects that he could control. One reason he preferred to be alone with his toys was that other kids weren't predictable. He never seemed to know what he could expect from them. Eric often felt powerless, and control became very important to him. But he quickly found that he couldn't dictate other kids' behavior the way he could manipulate his toys. Liane Willey, an adult with Asperger syndrome, says of her childhood,

> Maybe the desire to organize things rather than play with things was the reason I never had a great interest in my peers. They always wanted to use the things I had so carefully arranged. They would want to rearrange and redo. They did not let me control the environment. They did not act the way I thought they should act.[1]

Relationships are a negotiation between two people. If one party doesn't "speak the language" of compromise, his controlling ways will poison the budding friendship. No one wants to spend time with someone who won't meet him in the middle. The problem is, a spectrum kid genuinely doesn't know how to meet others in the middle. For this reason, he may tend to avoid his peers, finding it easier to interact with adults, because an adult will be more likely to adapt himself to him, smoothing over any social awkwardness, and not expect as much in return.

"READING" NONVERBAL COMMUNICATION

There's another very important reason that spectrum people find relating to others so challenging. Numerous studies have shown that they lack the natural ability to "read" a face or extract meaning from gestures, bodily stance, or tone of voice. This is a skill that typical kids begin mastering as babies.

We taught Eric the meaning of elementary facial expressions, vocal tones, and gestures by rote as part of his early intervention training. But because my face didn't impart any useful information to him, he didn't look at it often. He also didn't pay much attention to my tone of voice, gestures, or bodily stance. Although the early intervention training improved his understanding, we still had a long way to go.

Because spectrum kids don't pick up this information, they're less able to make an educated guess about how someone else is feeling and what he may want. This makes them less able to understand the other person's point of view. Spectrum people are also less likely to be able to form an empathetic connection to the other person, that is, to "feel with" him. This also may be related to their difficulty grasping the cues others get from faces, tone of voice, and gestures.

Spectrum people are often accused of being unloving, or of lacking compassion. One reason is that it's challenging for them to express themselves, particularly about their emotions. Another is that they find it hard to translate feelings into action. Some common complaints of typical women married to men with Asperger syndrome are, "He can't love me. He just ignores me." "If he loves me so much, why doesn't he ever say so?" "Why won't he help me if he loves me so much?"

Because your child has trouble seeing things from your point of view, it's hard for him to guess what you might need or want. He also won't recognize from your facial expression and tone of voice that you're unhappy, so he won't know that he needs to change his behavior to improve his relationship with you. This tendency can result in lost roommates, jobs, and marriages later in life.

PEER PROBLEMS

Spectrum kids can develop problem behavior patterns, particularly at school, because it's hard for them to understand others' feelings and intentions. Sean Barron was born during the sixties, long before any effective intervention for autism was discovered. He had a low level of function until his middle teens, but amazingly, today lives a fairly typical life. With his mother Judy, Sean wrote a courageously honest account of his very difficult childhood, describing how he felt, and why he did the things that he did. Here's an explanation of why Sean tended to isolate himself while at school.

> The playground was dangerous because the other kids were all around me, and they could do whatever they wanted to me. Now I realize that because I felt so negative about myself, I assumed that they would too and that they would try to hurt me. Although no one ever attacked me throughout grade school, I never lost my fear of being on the playground with the other kids, so I tried never to make eye contact with them.[2]

Spectrum kids not only misunderstand others in this way, they're also commonly misunderstood. The behavior Sean describes can easily be seen as hostile, particularly if it is accompanied by aggressive behavior. Peers can amuse themselves by taunting a child like this mercilessly. When pushed to the breaking point, spectrum kids often resort to hitting, because they lack the skills to resolve conflict any other way. And when adults try to referee a conflict involving a spectrum kid, because it's difficult to connect with him emotionally, he's often assumed to be the problem.

Classmates can also "set up" a naïve, compliant spectrum child to get in trouble, just to laugh at his credulity. Kids who have been treated like this sometimes begin to interpret even friendly overtures as threats, and accidents as deliberate. They also may retaliate for perceived insults. This tends to escalate the bullying and deepen their isolation.

JUST MAKING EXCUSES?

Does it sound to you as though I'm making excuses for behavior that, in a typical person, we'd just call selfish and sinful? I hope not! As I've mentioned throughout this book, God doesn't exempt spectrum people from obedience to His commands. Selfish behavior can become a tenacious besetting sin in a spectrum adult. So training your child to understand others better is only part of your job. The other part is constantly confronting him with Christ's claims on his life. The Lord calls all of us to be more attentive to others and place their needs ahead of our own. This may be harder for our spectrum children than it is for our typical kids, but God promises enough grace to meet any need His people may have.

But even as we urge our spectrum kids on to greater godliness, we should never lose sight of the fact that Christ has special compassion for struggling "weak sheep" (see Isaiah 40:11). And so as we seek to teach our spectrum kids to imitate Christ's compassion and patience, we need to do the same ourselves. "Love bears all things, believes all things, hopes all things, endures all things" (1 Corinthians 13:7).

SOCIAL SKILLS CAN BE EXPLICITLY TAUGHT

Not only does your child have difficulty reading the nonverbal signals of others, she also doesn't learn very well by observing social interactions involving others. This is probably because she doesn't understand what she's seeing. She won't pick up "unwritten rules" unless you teach them explicitly to her. But the good news is that once spectrum kids understand these rules, most follow them diligently.

> *I encourage you to work on increasing*
> *your child's involvement with others,*
> *even if he really prefers to be alone.*

Your child may or may not be interested in making friends. Many don't recognize why being with others is such a big deal, and prefer their own company and special interests. But all but the lowest-functioning kids will need people skills when they enter the working world. Doing all you can when your child is young to help him understand others as well as possible will help him prepare for his future.

Numerous studies have shown that even highly educated spectrum adults have difficulty selling themselves at job interviews. Once hired, they find it harder to keep their jobs. Much unemployment among adult autism spectrum people is due to a lack of people skills. So I encourage you to work on increasing your child's involvement with others, even if he really prefers to be alone. I'll suggest ways to do this in the next section.

Some higher-functioning kids will be very eager for the friendship of others. Some will even have enough insight to recognize that they are not accepted, and long to understand how to fit in better. These are the kids who will do the best in social skills training, because they're motivated to learn these skills. But any kid can improve if you are persistent in teaching him.

Dr. Temple Grandin, an older woman on the spectrum, tells a fascinating story of her social development from a severely autistic child to an entrepreneur with her own business (which is based upon her special interest in cattle). She's also a university professor of animal science. Temple is the author of a number of books, and speaks widely on autism. She says that she realized that lacking certain social skills was holding her back in her work, so she devoted herself to studying social interactions. This has greatly improved her ability to do her job and enjoy working relationships.

I first heard Temple speak fifteen years ago, and have followed her career since that time. I'm impressed by how much she's improved her interpersonal style over the years. Evidence of remaining spectrum tendencies has lessened as she's refined her social skills. Temple's story inspires me, because it shows that even spectrum adults approaching retirement age can continue to grow socially.[3]

HOW TO HELP YOUR CHILD LEARN SOCIAL SKILLS

Let's look at ideas for helping your child with social skills during three basic developmental stages: Preschool through kindergarten, primary through middle school, and high school through adulthood.

Preschool through Kindergarten

Eric was taught to share, take turns, and trade toys during his early intervention training. These were very important skills, because they taught him to relate as an equal with another child, rather than trying to make his playmate do what he wanted. As autism spectrum adult Jerry Newport says, "To share, you have to give up control."[4] One of the ways to woo your child into relinquishing control is to make "sharing practice" as fun as possible. You can invite a play partner over and act as the "play coach." This involves setting up interactions and praising lavishly for successful sharing, taking turns, and related skills. You may find that the typical play partner enjoys this even more than your child does. All little ones like having adults join them in play. You can also take your child and his play partner on outings.

In time your child may need less active coaching, and you can fade your assistance. But you'll probably find that he'll do better socially if you continue to act as a "play shadow," stepping in to help him when he becomes anxious or doesn't know what to do. I stayed close enough to know what was going on with Eric during his play dates for years so I could help whenever necessary.

I understand that not every parent has the time or inclination to do as much social skills training as their child needs. If this is your situation, you might consider starting your child in Floortime or RDI. These programs are discussed in appendix B.

Primary through Middle School

I found that I needed to keep taking the initiative to invite kids over to play as Eric entered the primary school years. I sweetened the offer with lots of opportunities to go special places and do unusual things. Eric did well with just one other kid, but when a third child was added he tended to isolate himself with his Game Boy while the other two played together.

It seems that having to interact with more than one friend at a time taxes a spectrum person's emotional resources, and when this happens they become anxious. Of course, an anxious spectrum kid is likely to either isolate or become angry. This is probably a big part of the reason why social situations at school can be such a challenge for your child. There are just too many kids, and there's too much social interaction to process.

These are the years when bullying and negative behavior patterns tend to develop at school. If your kid is attending, you'll want to be sure that his teachers understand the nature of his difficulties and are actively intervening. If he is mainstreamed, or in private school, I suggest that you also make sure that his school is taking active steps to educate his peers about his challenges.

If your child is in public school, she may be offered the opportunity to participate in social skills training. These groups can be very successful in teaching unwritten social rules. They can also help your child figure out what she's doing wrong when things don't go well with typical peers. Not all schools offer these groups, but it's important for your child to be in one if possible. If your school doesn't have such a program, I recommend that you take whatever steps you can to find her a group, even using private resources, if necessary. If your child is already doing RDI, social skills training will be a part of her program.

Social Skills Training at Home

Even if your child is in a social skills group, I suggest that you work on skills at home, too. This is a good time for him to learn greater sensitivity toward other family members. Because he isn't good at drawing conclusions about how people are feeling and what they need, he needs to learn to become comfortable with asking questions. Spectrum kids often stop asking questions if they've been called "stupid" at school. But because your child already has difficulty getting information from observation alone, failing to ask questions will keep him from learning things that he really needs to know. Home should be a safer place than school to practice this.

You can teach your child to ask regularly what she can do to help around the house, even when it doesn't seem to her as though there is any need. She should also learn to be comfortable asking if anything is wrong whenever she has the sneaking suspicion that she's missing something. Practicing these family communication skills will not only make life at home smoother for everyone, but they will help prepare her for the day when she may have roommates or a family of her own.

Your family needs to learn to communicate more explicitly with him, too. Don't expect him to discern from your behavior that he's said something hurtful, or ignored something important to you. If he doesn't get you a birthday card, tell him how that makes you feel. Tell him that his failure communicates that you're not important to him, and explain why receiving a card is important to you. If you relate this in an unemotional way, he'll receive it as information, not as condemnation. He probably won't make the same mistake again, either.

For Less Able Kids

If your child is less able than Eric was at this age, you may find that he doesn't have a friend yet. In this case, I recommend that you still try to keep him connected, although it may become more difficult to do. If it's hard to interest other kids in coming to your house, there's always church available as a social opportunity. If he still sits in the nursery or the "cry room" during the Sunday service, or if you're staying home to avoid bad behavior at church, a first step is to train him to sit in the sanctuary during the service. You may need to let your pastor know what you're trying to do and get his support, as the transition could be rocky for a while.

*Make sure he's included in church
events for kids his age, shadowing him yourself,
if necessary, to enable him to attend.*

Begin to practice sitting still while listening to a sermon on TV every day, correcting his behavior using the principles in chapters 2 and 3 as necessary. You can gradually increase the time he's able to sit quietly, and once he's ready, you can begin attending the service. Your goal is to get him to sit through a Sunday service and mingle with others afterward without melting down.

If your child needs a shadow to attend Sunday school and VBS, you may need to arrange this with your church's Sunday school director. You also may need to do the shadowing yourself, or to teach the class assistant how to do it. I suggest that you make sure he's included in church events for kids his age, shadowing him yourself, if necessary, to enable him to attend.

One of the reasons that it may be difficult to get typical kids to come to your home and on outings with your child is that they find your child's failure to connect awkward. But if you let your need be known around your church, there may be parents who will help their children push through their natural reluctance to love a different child, for Christ's sake. I've always urged Eric to visit kids with developmental challenges as a tangible way of showing the love of Christ to an isolated child. If you're the parent of a more able spectrum child, do consider encouraging your child to help others in this way, too.

Teen Years through Adult

These are very difficult years for most spectrum kids, regardless of how able they are. I've discussed the emotional challenges spectrum kids face in chapter 6. When you add the stresses of socializing, it puts many kids over the top emotionally. Even very high functioning spectrum teens will be a number of years behind their typical peers in their social and emotional development, and less able kids may fall further behind. There's a real danger that less socially successful kids may take refuge in bitterness, depression, and withdrawal. This can also result in serious challenges to their faith. More insightful spectrum kids may ask why God made them this way, and be angry with Him for their lack of social success. Unfortunately, they may also take this anger out on you, considering you a "safe" target who won't abandon them, unlike their classmates.

Brighter spectrum kids may take refuge in arrogance, fantasizing that they don't fit in because they are so superior. Some deliberately cultivate Mr. Spock's or Lt. Data's aloofness.[5] These kids may claim that they don't understand typical social interaction, and don't need to. There are even Web sites written by spectrum people that poke fun at neurotypical ways. Some have authored papers describing "neurotypical disorder."[6] These papers make it clear that spectrum people are deeply hurt by any implication that they are "abnormal" or unacceptable the way they are. And rightly so!

These spectrum adults object that they shouldn't have to adapt themselves to fit into a neurotypical world. But, of course, the Bible contests this claim. Christ calls all of us who are committed to Him to seek first His kingdom, not our own comfort or pride (Matthew 6:33). He taught that our goal as His disciples is to serve others, rather than insisting upon being the one who is served (Matthew 20:25–28). We are called to adapt ourselves to others for love's sake (1 Corinthians 9:22; 10:24). In calling autism spectrum people to the same kind of radical discipleship that He calls typical people to, He affirms their worth and equality in His sight. This is far from an attitude that sees spectrum people either as superior *or* as inferior!

Using superiority as a defense against fears of inferiority doesn't answer the deep human need to be accepted. Ultimately, your spectrum child must find his acceptance and sense of purpose in his relationship with the God who created him and has a plan for his life. I worked hard with Eric to cultivate his sense of being created by God with a specific purpose in mind, to counter the temptation of this kind of misplaced pride. Many of the concepts I shared in chapters 1 and 2 are the fruit of these discussions with Eric. Both of us learned to draw comfort and encouragement from the assurance that God made him the way he is for a reason and that He has a plan for Eric's life.

I also emphasized repeatedly the fact that adult life isn't anything like life in the average American high school. I urged Eric to work hard to prepare himself for his adult life, both intellectually and socially. During different times in his adolescence, he experimented with superiority, or was tempted by the urge to withdraw completely and only focus on his studies. But as time went on, he became willing to acknowledge his desire for relationship. Once he did this, he began asking me questions to discover where he was making social mistakes. And as he did, he grew.

YOUR CHILD'S MOST IMPORTANT RELATIONSHIP

Christian spectrum kids usually develop very deep, committed, trusting faith in childhood. But their emotional storms in adolescence can severely batter their faith. Once again, this isn't unique to our spectrum kids, but it's often much more intense with them. This underscores the special challenge your child may have transitioning from trusting, childlike faith to a personal, adult relationship with Jesus Christ. Because spectrum kids aren't good at building relationships, even with people they can see, growth in faith may take far longer for them than for typical kids. Let's talk about some ways you can help nurture your child's faith.

> *Continue to hold family devotions with him as long as he's willing to participate.*

It's important to teach all of our children, typical or spectrum, to be devoted to the disciplines of faith. Because your child becomes comfortable in places he knows well, and once committed tends to stay committed, attending church regularly from early childhood is important to build that bond in his life. Without consistency of attendance, he may be much less likely to consider the church an essential part of his life. Similarly, regular family devotions will do much to draw his heart toward simple faith in childhood.

You may be distressed to discover that your child prays the same brief, formula prayer every day during family devotions. This may not be an accurate index of the state of his deepest feelings, though. Remember that spectrum people find it difficult to put their thoughts into words. You can teach your child to develop and maintain a prayer list, and pray from it daily. This may help provide mental "scaffolding" upon which he can build more creative prayers as he matures.

Your child needs to have his own private prayer and devotions as he gets older, but I suggest that you also continue to hold family devotions with him as long as he's willing to participate. Because he may have difficulty envisioning and relating to God by himself, your example in prayer may make a big difference.

I've had to come to terms with the fact that I can't know the actual state of Eric's heart toward God. This is hard for me! I have to trust the Holy Spirit to do His work in my son's heart, whether or not I'm able to see obvious evidence of it. This drives me to be far more fervent in prayer than I was when Eric had the simple faith of a child.

Your child is on a different developmental path because of his differences, and his growth in faith may take significantly more time than it does for typical kids. Uncertainty about the state of your child's heart should drive you to prayer. As you pray for your child, you can have confidence that the gracious Lord who designed him will be faithful to complete the work He started in his life when he was small (Philippians 1:6). May He glorify Himself in your life and that of your child.

CHAPTER 8

Mad Elephants
AND MATURITY

"We have to release our children to follow their own vision."

MRS. JUMBO HAD BEEN PATIENT. She'd suffered silently when, after the stork brought her baby, the other elephants laughed at his big ears. She'd named him Jumbo Jr., but they called him Dumbo. He'd tripped over his ears during the circus parade and fallen into a mud puddle. The onlookers had laughed at him, and she still did nothing. But finally she'd had enough. She came upon a group of boys who were ridiculing him, became enraged, and spanked the cruelest boy with her trunk. The elephant handlers arrived and tried to restrain her, but she fought back with all her strength. She ended up locked away in a cage labeled "Danger! Mad Elephant."

THE WRONG KIND OF LOVE

I'm sorry to have to tell you that I've been there. I've been a "mad elephant," furious at the unkindness that Eric's peers were capable of, and heartbroken that the adults in his life didn't understand him as I did, either. I've let my love for Eric cause me to completely lose perspective, and forget that Christ calls me to seek first *His* kingdom, not my son's. I've failed to love brothers and sisters in

Christ as I should have because I was temporarily controlled by the wrong kind of love for my child.

What is this wrong kind of love? It's an instinctive desire to protect, one that doesn't consider the truth that God is in control in all the situations a child faces, and has a purpose, even in his suffering. It's a belief that the end justifies the means, and that the most important thing is helping my child, not glorifying God. It's mother love, and it's a work of the flesh (Galatians 5:19–20).

What do I mean by this? How could mother love be wrong? The Bible teaches that although mother love comes naturally to me, my instincts are tainted by my sinful nature, so they can't be relied upon to tell me the right way to respond. When I'm overwhelmed by anger, I'm yielding to what the Bible calls the "passions of the flesh" (1 Peter 2:11). I'm not making my choices about how to respond based upon biblical principles like not returning evil for evil (Romans 12:17), and communicating in a way that builds people up instead of tearing them down (Ephesians 4:29). When I feel overwhelmed by my anger and act out of it, I'm also failing to draw upon the Holy Spirit's resources, which God promises will enable me to overcome the temptation to do the wrong thing (1 Corinthians 10:13).

HELPING OR MANIPULATING?

Next in Dumbo's story, his friend Timothy Mouse tries to "fix" things for him. He thinks that Dumbo needs more self-esteem, so he manipulates behind the scenes to get Dumbo designated as the headliner in one of the circus acts. I've been there, too. I've not only helped Eric practice his social skills, but I've also manipulated situations to enable him to qualify for opportunities that he couldn't get by himself. Do I need to tell you that when Dumbo got his big chance as a headliner he tripped over those ears again? The other elephants were injured, the circus tent was torn down, and he was completely ostracized. Similarly, my manipulation sometimes caused more problems than it solved.

> *Would you just rather keep your baby home because it's easier on him and easier on you?*

Please understand me. I'm not telling you that the skills I've taught you in earlier chapters are manipulation. But there's a fine line between assisting your child in his social interactions and covering for his mistakes. There's a difference between helping your child gain his own social victories and getting them for him while ensuring that he gets the credit. In our efforts to make our children happy, we may actually be setting them up for ultimate failure. In our attempts to protect our children from suffering, we may be keeping them from experiencing consequences of their choices that they need to learn. I know I've crossed that line on some occasions. And I've crossed it because, at the moment of decision, I cared more about making my child happy than about glorifying God by walking in the truth.

I've made the opposite mistake too, at other times. Instead of pushing to get Eric included, sometimes I've tried to protect him from hurt by keeping him away from contact with other people. It wasn't hard to do. Eric didn't have a very strong social drive, and he didn't take the initiative to get together with other kids very often. I kept him close to me even though I knew that he needed social contact so he could learn. What was I afraid of? Sometimes I was afraid that he'd be hurt by the unkindness of others. I'm ashamed to admit that, at other times, I was afraid that I'd be criticized for my child's gaucheness and poor behavior.

WHAT'S YOUR STRUGGLE?

In which ways do you struggle? Are you tempted to demand full inclusion for your child even when his participation isn't really appropriate? Do you become an angry "mad elephant" when it doesn't work out? Have you been dishonest about your kid's abilities to get him accepted into a program that might not consider him if they knew the whole truth about his challenges? Or would you just rather keep your baby home because it's easier on him and easier on you?

Whether you tend to be too aggressive or too fearful, the good news is that you can take your failures to the cross and trust that Christ will give you the grace to start over tomorrow. Jesus Christ was the perfect blend of grace and truth (John 1:14). He can enable you to be gracious and merciful if your problem is that you tend to sacrifice kindness on the altar of expediency. He can give you the grace to speak the truth in love (Ephesians 4:15) if you tend to sacrifice honesty for mercy.

And even as I acknowledge my many failures, I'm encouraged to recognize that ultimately there's nothing I can do to prevent God from accomplishing His purposes in my son's life. We see this play out in Dumbo's story, too. After

Dumbo's failure as a headliner, Timothy Mouse is out of ideas. Dumbo's mother is locked up, unable to help him. But just when it seems that all is lost, Dumbo discovers that he can fly. Similarly, even when I'm out of ideas and it seems that there's no way to solve a problem, God is still in control. He *will* cause Eric to become the man that He created him to be. No power on earth, not even my sinful failures, can keep this from happening.

YOU MAY NEED TO GIVE UP SOME DREAMS

Here's another mistake I've made. Sometimes I've behaved as though it's up to me to be the Holy Spirit in Eric's life. I've tried to figure out what God wants to do with Eric's life and make it happen for him. I've sometimes crossed the line from helping him develop more appropriate interests, and instead have tried to map out his future exactly the way I thought it ought to be. Don't misunderstand me. It's a good thing to try to move your child from something that she's "stuck" on that is sapping her energy and keeping her from discovering other interests. But ultimately she's going to have to build a life that works for her—not the person that you want her to be. And the painful truth is that your child may not fulfill all the dreams you have for her, no matter what you do.

> *I had to learn when Eric was small*
> *that I couldn't control all of his social*
> *experiences and protect him from hurt.*

Some spectrum kids may not leave their stims and obsessions behind, no matter how hard you work on it. Such a young person may need help easing into employment, and may even require sheltered or shadowed work. Some higher-functioning spectrum kids, on the other hand, may be determined to live a life that their parents don't understand and find it hard to accept.

Either of these outcomes may be very difficult for you to accept. You have dreams for your spectrum child, just as parents of typical kids do. But even as parents of typical kids have to die to their own goals and trust God to do what's best in their children's lives, we do too. We have to release our children to follow their own vision.

And so I had to learn when Eric was small that I couldn't control all of his social experiences and protect him from hurt. When he began making his transition to manhood, I had to learn that he needed to build his own life for himself. I could offer guidance, I could help him consider options, but ultimately his progress was his own responsibility, and his destination was his to choose. Come to think of it, ultimately bringing a spectrum child to maturity isn't all that different from bringing a typical child to maturity, is it?

HELPING YOUR CHILD FIND HIS CALLING

So how can you help your child find his calling without putting yourself in the place of God and taking over? Well, for starters, don't make the opposite mistake and just step back and expect him to find his way all by himself. His interests may be pretty impractical, and he may not see himself objectively enough to be able to accurately gauge his strengths and abilities. For example, I knew a very inhibited young man with Asperger syndrome who wanted to major in theater at college. While I could see that he was interested because he wanted to understand others better, it was unlikely that he'd ever be able to make his living as an actor.

It's wise to help a teen who has an interest that may not be appropriate for future employment to develop other interests and abilities before he becomes too committed to the idea of pursuing his interest for a living. It might be possible to persuade someone like this young man to consider his interest in theater as a hobby that could enrich his spare time, but look to other strengths, such as math and science, as more fruitful sources of future gainful employment. Or perhaps he might be able to turn his scientific bent into a talent for theater lighting. If he's really interested in learning to understand people better through studying acting, he might consider a compromise major like interpersonal communications, which would enable him to learn many of the same things, but might be a better source of employment possibilities after graduation.[1] He could also minor, rather than major, in theater performance.

What about College?

What if your child doesn't seem to be college material? Many spectrum teens are able to attend community college if their behavior is controlled enough for them to be a mainstream student in a typical classroom by the time they graduate from high school. This is a great idea, even if your child isn't a strong student, because it gives him more time to grow in maturity while interacting with other young people in an educational setting before entering the adult world of work. Community colleges are also good sources of vocational training for specific careers.

Because the law requires that reasonable accommodations be made for people with disabilities, many community colleges and universities have disabled student centers that provide various services. Your child may qualify for additional time for taking tests, or for note-taking services or special tutoring through these centers. So don't be too quick to decide that college won't work for your child. If she does well in community college, transfer to a four-year college may even be a possibility. If that's too big a step, a community college vocational certificate or two-year diploma can provide her with the academic credentials to follow her interest into a rewarding career.

Some very high functioning spectrum young people gain direct admission to a university, as Eric did. If your child goes this route, it's good to know that disability services are often available on university campuses, too. If you think your child might find a university campus difficult, I suggest that you make sure that he chooses one that offers more than token help to spectrum people. You'll also want to consider whether he's ready to leave home and live in a dorm. If he hasn't done well socially in high school, living in a dorm on a large university campus may be a setup for failure. If this is the case, commuting to school from home may work better for him, as it did for Eric.

Other Employment Options

On the other hand, if your child truly hates school and hasn't discovered an academic strength yet, there may be no point in prolonging the agony. But I still recommend trying to find a vocational program for him so he can learn a skill, because it's going to be much harder for him to maintain employment without one. But I might encourage him in the direction of a shorter vocational course or apprenticeship, rather than a two-year community college program. Special interests can offer an opening to help your child develop related work interests. A teen who loves textures might enjoy learning to finish furniture or create pottery. Someone who enjoys doing detailed drawings might like draftsman training.

If your child is low functioning, she may need supported or shadowed employment. In this case, her special interests also may be more basic. But even these can be used to find a job that feels more natural and comfortable for her. For example, if she likes to line things up, some sort of assembly work (at a slow pace, like sheltered assembly for handicapped workers) might be enjoyable for her. She might find cleaning work that included arranging chairs in neat rows pleasant. The work environment would need to be slow-paced, quiet, and undemanding. You may be able to help your child find this kind of work privately, but often you'll need to take advantage of community resources to train and find employment for your child.[2]

THREE ADULT AUTISM SPECTRUM WORKERS

I'd like to introduce you to three remarkable spectrum adults. They range in function from high to low, but all three started life with autism, not the milder Asperger syndrome. Each one has used individual strengths to develop a fulfilling career, usually with the aid of parents or other adults who saw their potential and supported their aspirations. In two cases, their special interests led to a unique career. In the third, a young man has enriched his work environment with his diligence, faithfulness, and kindness. Each of these amazing spectrum adults has grown as a person in the context of his or her calling, and made their part of the world a better place by their contributions. Dr. Temple Grandin is an animal science professor and designer of humane slaughterhouses. Stephen Wiltshire is an autistic savant artist, and Jonathan Priebe is a workingman with autism who never takes a sick day.

Dr. Temple Grandin

Although I've already told you how Temple has grown in her understanding of people, there are many other wonderful things about her.[3] Temple started life severely autistic and mute. In the years before early intervention, children like Temple usually remained mute, but Temple's mother hired a nanny who worked with her to develop language. By the time Temple was four, she was speaking. But she had serious behavior problems throughout her childhood and, although bright, was an unmotivated student until she developed an interest that gave her a reason to study.

Temple spent summers at her aunt's cattle ranch as a teenager. She became obsessed with a machine called a squeeze chute that's used to restrain cattle for branding. She tried it on herself and found it helped her to calm her anxiety, and developed a modified squeeze chute for her own personal use.[4] This led to a desire to understand why the chute calmed cattle. Her high school science teacher encouraged her to bring up her grades so she could go to college and develop the tools to pursue this interest. This moved Temple to buckle down and master disciplines that didn't interest her, and her grades improved.

Temple thinks that if she hadn't found the squeeze chute comforting, she wouldn't have been motivated to learn how it worked. If she hadn't learned how it worked to calm cattle, she might not have begun to understand other things about them. Her understanding of cattle, in turn, led to the development of her unique work in slaughterhouse design.[5]

Temple says that she "thinks in pictures." By this she means that she can visualize things vividly.[6] This is a trait she shares with Albert Einstein, who had many autism spectrum characteristics and who claimed that his theory of relativity was born when he visualized riding on a beam of light through the universe. He then created mathematical equations that validated what he called his "thought experiment," and the rest is history.

Temple uses her visualization ability and her understanding of cattle to create slaughterhouse designs that keep the animals soothed until the moment they're sacrificed. Because of her emotional attachment to them, it's important to Temple that the cattle not suffer before their lives end. This attachment has motivated her to become an expert in her field.[7]

Temple didn't make a very auspicious start in life, and nobody could have been blamed for concluding that she wasn't very bright. Even in high school, she didn't really seem to be college material. But once she developed a strong interest, her drive to pursue it led to her achievements. Temple was also blessed with a mother who worked hard to understand her unique way at a time when no effective help from experts was available.

Stephen Wiltshire

Stephen started out even more autistic than Temple, and he continues to be fairly low functioning, in contrast to Temple, who is very high functioning today. But Stephen, like Temple, makes his living through his special interest, art.

Stephen began drawing in childhood. The drawings he did even when he was still a small child were like those done by a talented adult. This makes him an artistic prodigy. But because his baseline level of function is so low, he is also considered to be an autistic savant, someone who has an isolated area of unusual talent but has developed much more slowly than usual in other areas. For example, Stephen didn't speak until he was nine years old, and he couldn't cross the street alone until he was a teenager. This combination of child prodigy and autistic savant makes him a very unusual young man.

Stephen was blessed to have an art teacher at his school for developmentally challenged children who took a personal interest in him. This teacher nurtured Stephen's talent and took him to visit famous buildings, first in his native London, and later in other cities and countries. He also helped Stephen create an alphabet book based on London landmarks. This project was intended to encourage him to use language more by using his special interest, drawing buildings, as an incentive to speak. It was a creative idea, and one that increased Stephen's function significantly.

Numerous documentaries have been made about Stephen's abilities over the years, which have increased his renown.[8] Sir Hugh Casson, a former president of London's Royal Academy of Arts, once referred to Stephen as "possibly the best child artist in Britain." After Stephen left primary school and his teacher-mentor for secondary school, his talent languished for some years. But he was fortunate enough to be discovered later by an agent-mentor, who promoted Stephen's work, got commissions for him, and arranged for the publication of several books of his art, one of which was a national bestseller in Britain.[9] He was awarded the Order of the British Empire by Queen Elizabeth in 2006.

Now in his thirties, Stephen makes his living as a working artist. His art is displayed at a permanent gallery in a fashionable London neighborhood. Stephen lacks the initiative and entrepreneurial spirit of Temple, but his talent provides him with many opportunities. Stephen has also continued to develop in other areas. He has a real gift for mimicry, and in recent years has also developed a sense of humor. I understand that he can do a "wickedly accurate" imitation of singer Tom Jones, for example.

Dr. Oliver Sacks, who included essays about both Temple and Stephen in his book *An Anthropologist on Mars*, asks about Stephen, "(Are) there qualities, like autistic literalness and concreteness, that might in some contexts be gifts, in others deficits?"[10]

I don't like the use of the word *deficit* to describe autism spectrum traits. But Sacks's question is provocative in its suggestion that Stephen's adult identity is as much a consequence of his autism as it is of his artistic talent. All of the qualities that make Stephen, Stephen are gifts that enrich our world. Stephen is not a walking elephant—Stephen flies.

Jonathan Priebe

I was introduced to Jonathan via a YouTube video about him that was posted by his sister.[11] Jonathan's may just be the most remarkable of the three stories I'm sharing with you. You see, Jonathan's a workingman with autism. He's not a prodigy or a famous scientist. He's just a guy who goes to work every day and enriches his world because he's there.

Jonathan works in the supply department of the Grosse Pointe, Michigan, public school district. His job consists of filling requisitions from the various schools, boxing them, addressing the boxes, and loading them onto a truck for transport. Jonathan trained for his job for two or three years full-time, then for a while longer part-time, with a job coach who also taught his supervisor, Mike, how to work with him.

> *All our children can be helped to find an area where they can make a contribution by working **with** instead of **against** their natural inclinations.*

Mike says that Jonathan finds change difficult, so when it's necessary to alter his job routine, he calls Jonathan in advance to warn him. Jonathan had a lot of outbursts during his early days on the job, but this rarely happens anymore, because he's learned to manage his emotions better. Jonathan is a diligent and faithful worker. He never takes sick days and always gives his best effort. Mike says that everyone on the job loves Jonathan. He's friendly and makes a point of delivering homemade greeting cards to staff members on special occasions. "He has a heart of gold," says Mike. He adds that knowing Jonathan has enriched his life personally.

Jonathan's mother, Liz, emphasizes that her son is work-driven, rather than socially driven, so his work is central to his sense of identity. Unfortunately, because of cutbacks in the school district's budget, Jonathan's work hours recently have been decreased. Liz says, "Jonathan's success is still very tied to my perseverance," and points out that without her active involvement, he'll be unlikely to be able to regain full-time employment. She emphasized in an e-mail to me that adults with autism "have many contributions to make. They have skills and abilities that many of us don't have, and personal qualities that enrich the lives of people who know them. We need to find ways to let them make those contributions."

HELPING YOUR CHILD FIND HIS WORK

Obviously, all of our spectrum children aren't going to be gifted design engineers or artists. But all our children can be helped to find an area where they can make a contribution by working *with* instead of *against* their natural inclinations. We see this in the three stories I've just shared.

Reading Temple's story when Eric was still small caused me to ask myself how I might nurture his interests, in hopes that they might become areas of special ability as he matured. Most spectrum people have the ability to focus intensely upon the things that capture their attention, and most have an overwhelming drive to learn more about their special interest. These tendencies led Temple to make a unique contribution in her field—not in spite of her neurological differences, but *because* of them. We see similar drive in Stephen, who drew compulsively from childhood, and also took lessons in adulthood to refine his talent. Although he started out as a curiosity, a child who could draw buildings in detail from memory, his mature art is valuable for many other reasons besides the fact that he's autistic.

What's Jonathan's special interest? His work story doesn't tell us this. But it does tell us that he is a meticulous worker who is deeply committed to his job and rarely misses a day's work. We also learn that he is a kind and thoughtful coworker who enriches the lives of others. Even if your child's special interest doesn't result in an unusual talent like Temple's or Stephen's, he can still make important contributions to his world through his work, as a result of his unique character qualities. Remember Oliver Sacks's comment about Stephen. Your child's autism spectrum tendencies may themselves be the basis for a special contribution in the workplace, even as Jonathan's autistic attention to detail is probably the reason his work is so consistently excellent and he is so faithful to his job.

OUR ROLE AS MENTORS

A common feature in all three of these workers' stories is the central role of mentors, encouragers, and parents. It's probably true that none of us achieve our adult place in life without many mentors and encouragers. But this seems to be especially important for autism spectrum people. We see that all three of these people received special help from mentors. Temple's career became self-sustaining over time. Stephen has a drive to create art, but continues to lack the initiative and ability to run his own business. So he needs support to make his living from his art. Jonathan needed his mother's initiative, his job coach's training, and his supervisor's cooperation to allow his special qualities to shine at work.

This brings us back to where we started at the beginning of this chapter. As we seek to help our autism spectrum children find their way into meaningful careers, we probably will need to offer them special help. But we must not place helping our child ahead of honoring Christ and become "mad elephants." We also need to understand that our child's dream may not be what we would have chosen for him, and he may not pursue it in the way that we think best. If his career doesn't become self-sustaining, we may have to continue to provide direction and support well into adulthood, which may not be how we wanted to spend our retirement years. In all these things, let's fix our minds on seeking "first the kingdom of God and his righteousness" (Matthew 6:33), instead of our own goals or our child's advancement. We can trust the Lord to make a way for our children as we look to Him in faith.

CHAPTER 9

For This
CHILD I PRAYED

"What a privilege it's been to raise him up in
the discipline and instruction of the Lord."

I WAS THIRTY-SIX YEARS OLD, and desperate for a baby. I'd
longed to be a mother since childhood, but my medical training had postponed
my dream. Now I'd been married for a year, and had miscarried three times.
Would I never hold a child from my own body in my arms?

I'll admit it; in those days God didn't come first in my life. I wanted to do
His will, but only if it agreed with my desires. And I wanted a baby. Suddenly
I remembered. Hadn't a woman in the Old Testament prayed for a child? Yes,
it was Hannah, the mother of the prophet Samuel. She prayed, "[If you] will
give to your servant a son, then I will give him to the Lord all the days of his life"
(1 Samuel 1:11).

Little did I know what I was asking for as I prayed Hannah's prayer! But
two weeks later I knew I was pregnant, and nine months after that, a beautiful
son was laid in my arms. And as if God was emphasizing the special nature of
Eric's conception, I miscarried again with my next pregnancy. We would not
have another child.

I often dreamed of my "little Samuel's" future. Would he be the next Luther
or Calvin? A pioneer missionary whom God would use to do great things?

Maybe a scientist who would make a brilliant scientific breakthrough? Surely he would be remarkable. And so he was—just not in the way that I'd imagined.

When Eric was diagnosed with autism, they told us that he was retarded and would probably never speak. My heart screamed, *No! I gave him to You, God! You gave me a miracle! He was going to serve You all his life! How can he know You if he never understands what I tell him about You? How can he serve You if he never speaks?*

It was a dark period for my faith, but in time I came to understand that my hopes for Eric had been proud and self-centered. I'd wanted to be the mother of a great man. God wanted me to grow in faith as I walked through the death of my dream with confident trust in His goodness. Finally, by His grace, God enabled me to say, "Lord, even if Eric never speaks, I'll do everything I can to teach him to trust You. I'll raise him to serve You to the best of his ability. If You want him to glorify You as a nonverbal, mentally challenged, autistic man, I'll trust You to do just that in his life, and believe that it will be a good thing."

As you've learned throughout this book, I did everything I could to help Eric grow to his fullest potential. But I also trusted God to glorify Himself in Eric's life even if his potential turned out to be very limited. God used Eric's challenges in my life to cause me to grow in faith. I don't believe that I'd have become the woman I am today if He hadn't brought Eric into my life. What a privilege it's been to raise him up in the discipline and instruction of the Lord! Although I thought that his diagnosis was the worst thing that could possibly happen, it's turned out to be a source of some of the greatest blessings I've ever experienced.

Please don't get the idea from this story that I'm some kind of giant of faith, or that I've never experienced the feelings you have as the parent of a spectrum child. It hurt me profoundly to be the mother of an autistic boy! I mourned for the things that Eric wouldn't be, because of his differences. Oh, I did believe that God would glorify Himself in Eric's life, and I learned to trust Him to do it. And, yes, ultimately I had the joy of seeing Eric overcome the pessimistic expectations the doctors had given us. But this doesn't mean that I didn't miss, and don't still mourn for, many of the lovely little joys that mothers of typical kids take for granted, but that I never experienced with Eric. It doesn't mean that I don't continue to grieve as I watch Eric struggle to make his way in a world that still doesn't always understand and appreciate him. This is why, even today, I still love Hannah's story. Let me tell you more about her, and perhaps you'll see why her story is so precious to me.

GOD'S WORK IN HANNAH'S LIFE

Hannah suffered, as I had. We remember her for her prayer of faith, which gave Israel that great man of God, the prophet Samuel. But we may not realize that Hannah's life wasn't easy, either before *or after* her prayer. Before she prayed, she suffered the stigma of infertility, which was the worst shame that a wife in Israel could endure. On top of that, she bore the ridicule of her husband's second wife, who taunted her for her failure to conceive. After Hannah prayed, God did grant her request, but even then she didn't get to live happily ever after with her precious son. To fulfill the vow she'd made, she had to take him to the tabernacle of the Lord in Shiloh and leave him there when he was little more than a baby.[1]

Shiloh was a long way from Hannah's home. The Bible story tells us that she saw Samuel once a year after that.[2] God gave Hannah five more children, but how she must have missed her firstborn! How bittersweet Samuel's birth must have been for her—bitter, because she didn't get to raise him herself, but sweet because God had removed the stigma of her infertility.

Hannah's story inspires me because of her faithful response to her suffering. The Bible tells us that when Hannah delivered Samuel to the tabernacle in Shiloh, it was a time of rejoicing, not of grief. Isn't that remarkable? Can you imagine how you would feel if you were about to leave your baby with strangers, far away from your home? How could you face knowing that you'd only see him once a year after that? You certainly wouldn't feel like throwing a party, but that's just what Hannah did. She worshiped the Lord by sacrificing a bull, which was a very expensive offering for one family to make, and then she brought Samuel to Eli, and gave him to the priest. Hannah said,

For this child I prayed, and the Lord has granted me my petition that I made to him. Therefore I have lent him to the Lord. As long as he lives, he is lent to the Lord.

1 SAMUEL 1:27–28

And then, even more amazingly, Hannah offered a jubilant song of thanksgiving! Bible scholars think that Mary, the mother of Jesus, modeled her magnificent song of praise to God, which glorified Him for the great salvation He was accomplishing through her divine Son's birth, on Hannah's song of praise. Hear what God taught Hannah through her infertility and subsequent conception—yes, I daresay, even through her grief:

Those who were full have hired themselves out for bread,
   but those who were hungry have ceased to hunger.
The barren has borne seven,
   but she who has many children is forlorn.
The Lord kills and brings to life;
   he brings down to Sheol and raises up.
The Lord makes poor and makes rich;
   he brings low and he exalts.
He raises up the poor from the dust;
   he lifts the needy from the ash heap
   to make them sit with princes and inherit a seat of honor.
For the pillars of the earth are the Lord's,
   and on them he has set the world.
He will guard the feet of his faithful ones,
   but the wicked shall be cut off in darkness,
   for not by might shall a man prevail.

1 SAMUEL 2:5–9

Do you see what Hannah learned through her suffering? She learned that we can't get what we long for by our own strength, but God delights to exalt the weak and make them strong. Hannah could have become bitter because of the lot the Lord ordained for her life. It could have seemed unfair to Hannah, first to be infertile, and then to be set free from the shame of her infertility only through the sacrifice of her precious son. I know that I often struggled with this same sense of unfairness in the early days after Eric's diagnosis. But instead Hannah chose to glorify the Lord for the way He exalts the godly and punishes the wicked. She chose to believe that God was doing something good in her suffering, and to praise Him for it, even though she didn't yet understand why He had ordained the events that He had.

> *I don't know what's at the end of the road*
> *for your child, but I know that somehow,*
> *each in his own way, every one of our*
> *autism spectrum children will soar.*

Did Hannah live long enough to see the great man that her son became? Did she finally understand what God was doing through the things she had to suffer? Or did she die in faith, trusting that the Lord would make His purposes clear to her in His time? The Bible doesn't answer these questions.

GOD'S WORK IN MY LIFE

God has taught me similar lessons, through all the disappointments I experienced as the mother of a spectrum child. He's shown me that everything He does is good, even when I don't understand. He's taught me to wait in faith, believing that when He finishes accomplishing His purposes in my life, I'll agree that what He's done is for the best. I've come to understand that even those born weak and unimpressive can soar by His power. Hear what the prophet Isaiah says about those who trust in the Lord:

> *He gives power to the faint,*
> *and to him who has no might he increases strength.*
> *Even youths shall faint and be weary,*
> *and young men shall fall exhausted;*
> *but they who wait for the Lord shall renew their strength;*
> *they shall mount up with wings like eagles;*
> *they shall run and not be weary;*
> *they shall walk and not faint.*
>
> ISAIAH 40:29–31

Eric, who started life as a weak and stumbling "Dumbo," now soars by God's strength. I don't know what's at the end of the road for your child, but I know that somehow, each in his own way, every one of our autism spectrum children will soar. And you, dear parent, will see it and rejoice!

GOD'S WORK IN SAMUEL'S LIFE

Samuel must have suffered, too. He was a little boy, raised at the tabernacle of the Lord by priests. The Bible tells us that Samuel slept by himself in the temple.[3] I wonder why. Perhaps because he'd been dedicated to God, the temple itself had to be his home. Whatever the reason, this living arrangement couldn't have been very conducive to Samuel finding a close relationship with a woman who could take the place of his mother. Instead, it sounds as though Eli raised him. To be raised by the high priest himself, trained to serve God from early childhood, was a tremendous privilege. And yet it came at the terrible cost of separation from his loving mother and a normal family life.

Perhaps because of Samuel's unusual upbringing, he became one of Israel's greatest prophets, as well as her last judge. God honored Samuel by giving him his first prophecy when he was still a boy, and continued to reward him with the respect and loyalty of Israel throughout his life. Under his leadership, God's people put away their false gods and served only the Lord.

Samuel obeyed and honored God, even when the call on his life required significant self-denial and disappointment. Did he learn to deny himself to serve God through the lessons he learned as a boy, denied access to the comforts of home that he must have longed for? Perhaps this was part of God's perfect preparation for the unique role that Samuel would play in the history of Israel. Probably few servants of the Lord grew up with such a concentrated exposure to God's Word, and such an understanding of what a life of obedience to the Lord required. Did this make him a more effective prophet and judge?

Think of what God required of Samuel in his unique ministry. He was the greatest of the judges. He and all Israel naturally assumed that his sons would follow in his footsteps. But they didn't serve the Lord, so God commanded him to anoint Saul as the first king of Israel. Samuel must have been sorely disappointed, but there's no evidence that he resented God's decision, or objected to having to anoint someone else as king. Instead, he obeyed without arguing, and even worked faithfully to teach Saul to be an obedient king. In fact, he even must have learned to love Saul, because the Bible tells us that Samuel grieved over him when he fell from faith (1 Samuel 15:35). However, once again, he didn't argue or complain but obediently anointed David to replace Saul when commanded to. Samuel died long before David began his glorious reign in Jerusalem, so he didn't get to see the ultimate result of his life of dedicated service to God.

PREPARED FOR SERVICE THROUGH SUFFERING

It's clear that God had a unique plan for Samuel's life, one that required unusual dedication and obedience. He prepared Samuel for his future from early childhood through the intensive discipleship he received from Eli. This demanding training required the denial of the comforts of hearth and home, things that most of us would say are essential to produce a healthy, happy adult life. God raised up an exceptional servant, and He did it, at least in part, through suffering.

> *I know that I asked God,*
> *"Why me?"*

And so we see, embedded in the pages of my favorite Bible story, a tale of two people, mother and son, both called by God to experience significant disappointments in their lives. Did either of them ever ask Him why they had to suffer the loss of things that most people are blessed to be able to take for granted, like easy conception, raising your child yourself, growing up with a mother in the home, and experiencing the joy of watching your children and others you've trained walk in obedient faith? Scripture is silent about whatever personal struggles they may have had, and only records how they glorified Him through their obedience, and through their worship.

ASKING "WHY?"

I know that I asked God, "Why me?" I wanted to know why other mothers got to have wonderful moments with their infants, cooing and smiling, basking in all that glorious mother-child love, while my baby was as unresponsive as a sack of potatoes most of the time. I wanted to know why other mothers of small children got grubby handfuls of dandelions and homemade love gifts, while the only way I received anything like this was if I first explained to Eric why it was important, and then helped him to pick the flowers or make the gift.

I also wanted to know why Eric had to suffer. I wanted to know why he had to experience all the disappointments and failures that came about through no fault of his own, because he didn't see the world the way other people do. I wanted to know why he had to miss out on so much that other kids never thought twice about having—the sports successes, the friendships, the appreciation of important adults in his life.

Here's why Hannah's and Samuel's stories have so much meaning for me. Hannah and Samuel didn't understand while they were going through their own disappointments and losses, any more than I understood, what God was doing through their sufferings. But God gave them the experiences that they had, and recorded them so that we could learn faith lessons from their lives. How do I know this? The Bible itself teaches that this is one reason its stories are recorded for us (see 1 Corinthians 10:11).

GOD HAS A PLAN

What did I learn from Hannah's and Samuel's lives? I learned that God's purposes for my life, and for my son's life, could well be bigger than simply giving us what would make us happy. Hannah and Samuel suffered so that I, and countless other believers like me, could learn from their endurance how God uses the lives of those who trust in Him.

> *"For I know the plans I have for you,*
> *declares the Lord, plans for wholeness and*
> *not for evil, to give you a future and a hope."*

They also suffered so that God could bring about His plans for Israel during that period of her history. Their suffering had a purpose. It wasn't meaningless. It was designed by God to accomplish good, not only in their own personal lives, but also in the larger world of their time, and as a legacy for believers, like me, yet to be born.

Jeremiah 29:11 says, "For I know the plans I have for you, declares the Lord, plans for wholeness and not for evil, to give you a future and a hope." As I look at Samuel's life, remembering not only the great purposes God accomplished for the nation of Israel through his ministry but also the good He did in Samuel's personal life through his suffering, I can be confident that God is doing the same for Eric. Romans 8:28–30 tells us,

> *And we know that for those who love God all things work together for good, for those who are called according to his purpose. For those whom he foreknew he also predestined to be conformed to the image of his Son, in order that he might be the firstborn among many brothers. And those whom he predestined he also called, and those whom he called he also justified, and those whom he justified he also glorified.*

This passage tells us the good that God is doing in Eric's and my lives is about making us like Jesus Christ, and bringing us to eternal glory in Him. That's the ultimate purpose for which He's called us to Himself, which He will complete when we join Him to live in eternity forever.

Hannah and Samuel died in faith, perhaps without seeing any of the purposes God had for their lives come to fulfillment. Maybe neither of them was ever able to say, "Wow! So that's why that happened!" But in eternity, surely they know and rejoice in what God has done through their lives.

Similarly, God may call me to die in faith, trusting that He's fulfilled His plan for my life, even if I still can't see it at the time of my death. I also may not understand on this side of eternity all the reasons He had for creating Eric the way He did. If Eric continues to have various difficulties throughout his life, this won't mean that God isn't doing anything special in his life. He doesn't have to make Eric a success in the world's eyes for me to believe that He created him for a reason, and that He's doing something wonderful through his life, because I know that God has promised that this is what He'll do, and He always keeps His promises.

It's the same for your child, dear parent. If your child is still young, you have a lot of walking by faith to do before you'll get to the place I am now—and I've just said that I don't have all the answers. I know that you probably wanted to finish this book with faith and confidence, having heard me say that, in the end, your child will succeed in life. But some parents will have children who won't fulfill their hopes—either because they won't progress as much as they'd hoped, or because they'll remain low functioning, despite their parents' best efforts.

If this happens, does it mean that your child's life is pointless, or that the things you've suffered have no meaning? By no means! As you walk by faith, you're glorifying God through that very action. And as your child walks by whatever light that God has given him, he glorifies God, too.

OUR ETERNAL HOPE

Don't forget that this life is not all that there is. Even if your child lives a very low-functioning life, at the moment of her death she will be perfectly "conformed to the image of [God's] Son" (Romans 8:29). This means she will perfectly reflect the image of God, which, like the rest of us, she reflects only imperfectly in this life. At the moment she joins the Lord in heaven, she'll fulfill the ultimate purpose for which she was created. And that's not all. One day, at the end of time, your child will rise from the dead in a perfect, glorified body. She'll be incapable of sinning, or of any physical imperfection, from that point on for all eternity!

This reminds me, once again, of Hannah's song. Hannah didn't sing her song because she got a happy ending in this life. God's plan for her child necessitated a permanent separation from him. Surely honoring her promise led to acute suffering on her part. It led to suffering for her son, too. And yet she sang. Why? Hannah sang for joy at the glorious truth that God brings down the proud and raises up the lowly, and how she'd seen that happen in her own life. Not all spectrum kids will achieve typical function in this life. But all will live forever as typical glorified saints in the new heavens and new earth, where there will be no more sin, pain, sickness, or developmental challenge. Dear believing parent, wait in faith for that day!

APPENDIX A

"Is My Child on THE AUTISM SPECTRUM?"

YOU MAY HAVE PICKED up this book not because your child has been diagnosed with an autism spectrum disorder, but because you're wondering if he might have one. I've met a number of parents recently who've read about Asperger syndrome, and have concluded from what they've read that their child has it. And in some cases they've been wrong. For this reason, I encourage parents who are worried about their children to begin by having a full evaluation of him or her done by an expert in autism diagnosis. Because autism treatment is most effective when it begins as early as possible, this evaluation should take place as soon as possible.

Your pediatrician may have already made a diagnosis and referred you to your public school or local regional center for treatment. But I recommend that you first get your child evaluated by experts at a university or children's hospital developmental disorders clinic. You can ask your pediatrician to write you a referral to the nearest specialty center like this in your area. The center should do a full speech and language assessment, and a developmental assessment. Imaging studies, EEG, and blood tests may also be done. Once you understand the full scope of your child's challenge, you'll be better equipped to get the best possible help for her. This will help you to know how extensive her treatment should be.

But what if you haven't even talked to your pediatrician yet? Maybe you're afraid that he'll think you're a nervous mother if you express your concerns. Perhaps you're hoping that there's really nothing to be worried about, and that the situation will resolve by itself. Boy, do I remember struggling with feelings like that! That's why I wanted to include this appendix—both to reassure you if there really isn't anything to be concerned about, and to get you going in the right direction if there is. This is important because the sooner your child is diagnosed, the sooner that all-important early intervention training can begin.

HOW OLD MUST MY CHILD BE BEFORE A DIAGNOSIS CAN BE MADE?

On the one hand, there's no point in worrying about an infant. Many children under one year of age have phases of difficult or unusual behavior, which naturally pass with time. On the other hand, suppose your pediatrician tells you that he wants to wait another six months to see if your nonverbal two-year-old's language develops on its own—this isn't a good idea. Experienced autism experts can diagnose autism in an eighteen-month-old, in most cases. So if your pediatrician isn't sure, and you're worried, asking for a referral to an autism diagnosis center is the best way to go. If your child has autism, his best chance for improvement will be between the time he is diagnosed and his fourth birthday. For this reason, it's just not wise to wait.

WHAT ARE SOME EARLY SIGNS OF AUTISM?

Some babies who will later be diagnosed with autism don't appear unusual in any way. Others cause their parents concern almost from birth. I remember the first time they placed Eric in my arms as though it were yesterday. My very first thought was, *Dear Lord! He's autistic!* To this day I can't tell you why I thought this. I was a first-time mother, but as the oldest daughter in a large family I'd had a lot of experience with babies. There was just something different about him. I didn't mention my concerns to anybody. There was no point in doing so, since I couldn't give a reason for the way I felt.

Although I tried to tell myself that, as a psychiatrist in training, I just had "medical student syndrome" (a tendency to think you have whatever disease you are currently studying), I was never really able to shake the fear that something was wrong with Eric. For one thing, he was an unusually placid child. In fact, he literally *never* cried. I used to say that if I forgot to feed him, he'd starve to death, because he never seemed to be hungry. But he ate whatever I gave him enthusiastically and gained weight normally.

At the other behavioral extreme, the late Dr. Bernard Rimland, founder of the Autism Research Institute, told me that his son would scream inconsolably unless his wife always wore the same dress when she held him. She ultimately purchased several identical dresses and wore them all the time to try to keep him calm. This is another common pattern in young autistic babies, the tendency to be extremely irritable and crave sameness.

Eric didn't seem to care whether I held him. He was content to lie alone, staring at the ceiling all day. If I took him for a walk in his carriage, he wouldn't sleep like most new babies do, but was unusually alert, transfixed by the shifting shadows he could see through the sunshade. What was really disturbing was that he was fascinated by those shadows, but he wasn't at all interested in my face. He didn't respond when I talked to him, and he didn't make answering noises in return. He didn't mind my playing peekaboo or patty-cake with him, but it didn't seem to thrill him the way it did other babies. He also didn't develop stranger anxiety, as most babies do, around a year or so of age. He'd go to anyone without a complaint, and he didn't seem to notice if I left him.

Eric's large motor milestones were all delayed. They weren't so late as to cause his pediatrician concern, but I'd be holding my breath waiting for him to finally sit up alone, or pull up to a standing position. He never tried to walk around the room in his walker the way other babies did, but sat still in it. I didn't need child locks for my kitchen cabinets, because he never tried to open them. But he would crawl over to his stroller and try to spin its wheels for hours. If I tried to read a book to him, he'd pull it out of my hands and throw it across the room. But by the time he was a year old, he loved to sit by himself, turning the delicate pages of the telephone book one by one. He never tore one.

WHAT ARE SOME SIGNS OF AUTISM IN TWO-YEAR-OLDS?

Probably the most noticeable difference in the second year of life is that a spectrum child isn't speaking, or isn't speaking normally. In his first year of life, Eric didn't babble, but in his second year he began to make meaningless speech-like sounds and connect them together in what sounded like sentences. Experts refer to this speech-like vocalizing as "jargon." Eric also occasionally repeated a word I spoke, which experts call "echolalia." But there was no evidence that he understood what the word he was repeating meant, and he never used it appropriately to refer to anything.

Recent research suggests that toddlers who speak in jargon and display echolalia are less able to understand speech. In other words, they imitate speech sounds, but without understanding why we make them. I remember someone telling me, "I don't think Eric understands a word I'm saying." I was sure he was wrong. But when Eric finally had his speech and language evaluation at the age of thirty months, they told us that he understood less spoken language than the average three-month-old.

Another equally important difference you'll notice is in your child's social relatedness. It's not just that he isn't speaking, it's that he doesn't seem to have any pressing desire to communicate with you. Eric not only didn't point at things that interested him, he didn't look when I pointed things out to him. In fact, he didn't seem to understand what I was doing when I'd point to things. He also didn't look at me when I spoke to him. A study by Simon Baron-Cohen and colleagues suggests that if pointing behavior and reciprocal eye contact are absent at eighteen months of age, it is very likely that the child has autism.[1]

The Checklist for Autism in Toddlers (CHAT), a screening instrument that your pediatrician might use, asks the following questions that may be helpful for you to determine if your child has differences in his social relatedness:

1. Does your child enjoy being swung, bounced on your knee, etc.?
2. Does your child take an interest in other children?
3. Does your child like climbing on things, such as stairs?
4. Does your child enjoy playing peekaboo and hide-and-seek?
5. Does your child ever pretend play, for example, pretending to make tea with a toy teapot, and pretend to drink it?
6. Does your child ever point to something with his index finger, to ask for it?
7. Does your child ever point to something with his index finger, to indicate interest in it?
8. Can your child play properly with small toys (e.g., cars or blocks) without just mouthing, fiddling, or dropping them?
9. Does your child ever bring things to you to show them to you?

If the answer to a number of these questions is no, you should definitely consider asking your pediatrician if your child can be evaluated by an autism expert.

WHAT ARE EARLY SIGNS
OF ASPERGER SYNDROME?

More and more autism specialists are coming to the conclusion that Asperger syndrome is a higher-functioning variant of autism. What this means is that the symptoms are milder, and may not be recognized as early as the symptoms of autism, but they will be similar in type. This means that there will be challenges in the areas of speech and social relatedness, but they won't be as severe and obvious as they are in autism.

In the area of speech, your Asperger child may have no speech delay, or he may start speaking late, but do so on his own. He may have subtle difficulties with understanding the speech of others, and subtle differences in his own ability to put his thoughts into words. He may read fluently at an early age, but with poor understanding. Or he may speak fluently, using words that are advanced for his age, but use them oddly, or inaccurately. He may tend to "talk at" you rather than engaging in true conversation, and his speech may have a stilted, formal quality. Asperger kids are often described as "little professors" for this reason.

In the area of social relatedness, there will be poor eye contact, and some of the same kinds of concerns that the CHAT questions address. Your child may be interested in and may attempt to play with other children, but his efforts may be clumsy and ineffective. The result may be that he fails to connect with his peers and doesn't develop friendships.

Because Asperger challenges are subtler, it's not uncommon for parents not to realize that something is different about their children until they start school, at which time they may be told that their child's teacher suspects Asperger syndrome.

WHAT ARE SIGNS OF AUTISM
AND ASPERGER SYNDROME IN OLDER KIDS?

Repetitive actions, stims, and special interests are pretty universal in older autism spectrum kids, as are meltdowns and relationship difficulties. In addition, many autism spectrum kids have poor imaginative play, poor understanding of nonverbal cues, and difficulty understanding why certain behaviors are inappropriate. They may be overliteral in their understanding of things that they are told, and rigidly adhere to the "letter of the law," while failing to understand the reasons for rules. They also tend to resist change.

There are also differences in the way autism spectrum kids move. Autistic kids may be physically very graceful, while Asperger kids may be clumsy. Interestingly, Eric was graceful and fearless as a young autistic child, but as he advanced along the spectrum with age, he became more clumsy and fearful of falling. I remember the time that Eric followed his father up a ladder, onto the roof of our house, when he was two. His dad found him wandering alone fearlessly, close to the edge. But a few years later he was afraid of heights, and would fall while riding his bike, even with training wheels. He was eight before he could ride it without them.

Other spectrum kids may have an odd walk. They may walk on their toes, or without swinging their arms. Their running may be clumsy and slow. They may go up and down stairs placing both feet on each step, long after other kids their age are able to alternate their feet. Many have odd postures. You may recall the odd tilt of the head and gait in Dustin Hoffman's portrayal of Raymond, an autistic adult, in the movie *Rain Man*.[2]

DIAGNOSING ASPERGER SYNDROME IN ADULTS

You may know someone who was diagnosed with Asperger syndrome in adulthood. Their difficulties may not have been noticed in childhood, or they may have been noticed but not recognized for what they really were. But mere social awkwardness alone is not sufficient to make this diagnosis. There should be a history of other difficulties of the sort that I've mentioned here.

If you should realize in retrospect that your adult child has had difficulties in the past like I've described, it may be possible for her to benefit from social skills training or other help in adulthood. For this reason, persuading her to get an evaluation by an autism expert may be helpful to her. Even if she is not willing to be evaluated, if you recognize her difficulties as a result of reading this book, you may be able to use the principles I've taught you to help her, even in adulthood.

There are also women who've become convinced that their husbands have Asperger syndrome, sometimes after their child is diagnosed. Autism spectrum disorders do tend to run in families, but this doesn't mean that if you have an autistic child, you or your husband must have an autism spectrum disorder. But some very high functioning people with Asperger traits do marry. Marriages in which one partner has Asperger traits can be challenging. A wife who thinks her husband has Asperger syndrome may not be able to get him to agree to seek help for it, but some of the principles presented in this book can be adapted to make married life run smoother.[3]

May the Lord bless you with wisdom as you seek to help your autism spectrum loved one of any age.

Selecting a
TREATMENT PROGRAM

I RECOMMEND A FULL-TIME ABA early intervention program for all children diagnosed with autism in the preschool years. Many studies have demonstrated that ABA is effective in teaching new skills and reducing problem behavior. A number of studies additionally indicate that when ABA is provided intensively, before four years of age, it may produce large gains in development, as it did for Eric. There is no other early intervention program for autism that has been the potential to produce improvement like this. You can arrange for your child to receive ABA early intervention via a private program, or through your public school.

PRIVATE FULL-TIME ABA

Private ABA is an expensive option, but the one that is most likely to produce the greatest improvement in autistic children under the age of four. Your city may have a clinic that offers an ABA program directed by a Board Certified Behavior Analyst (BCBA). Studies have shown that for your child's program to be optimally effective, it must provide more than thirty-five hours a week of pure ABA for two years. Many clinics offer a combination of ABA and other treatments. You should be aware that only pure ABA programs produce the most dramatic gains.

Those who live in locations without a clinic can contact the Lovaas Institute[1] to arrange to have a BCBA travel to their home to set up an early intervention program. The Lovaas Institute also has treatment centers in a number of cities nationwide. Dr. Ivar Lovaas, who directed Eric's ABA program at UCLA in the early 1990s, is the creator of the ABA approach. I recommend the Lovaas Institute as a quality provider of ABA services.

Depending upon what kinds of services are available in your public school system, you may also be able to persuade your district to pay for your child to receive private ABA services. Some families have been successful in arguing that, as the law promises a "free, appropriate" education for disabled children, the public school district should provide funding for private ABA training if their schools don't offer it. They cite the scientific consensus that ABA is the most appropriate treatment for children with autism.

PUBLIC SCHOOL EARLY INTERVENTION SERVICES

Many parents choose to have their child receive early intervention services through their local public school. Typically, a child in a public early intervention program will receive some ABA, but it will be less than the thirty-five hours a week that has been linked to the best outcomes. A public school early intervention classroom will also include a number of children, rather than providing the exclusive, full-time, one-on-one attention that pure ABA programs emphasize.

Generally, the program will be run by a special education teacher rather than by a BCBA. Many teachers like to modify the ABA protocols to make them work better in a special education classroom, which could decrease their effectiveness. We don't really know, because "hybrid" programs like this haven't been studied.

Your child's program could also include occupational, physical, and speech therapy, in addition to the ABA. These are valuable services that should be offered to school-age children in special education classrooms. But in the early intervention years, the treatment most likely to produce gains is pure ABA. For this reason I recommend that you look carefully at your public school's program before deciding to place your child there.

TEACCH

TEACCH (Treatment and Education of Autistic and related Communication-handicapped Children) is an early intervention and special education program created by Dr. Eric Schopler, a North Carolina child psychiatrist. It is a well-respected program that has been in operation since the 1970s, and has been experimentally proven to be beneficial. But it doesn't offer the same potential for dramatic gains in the early intervention years as ABA. TEACCH[2] offers educational support through adulthood for autism spectrum individuals, including assisted employment, making it a very attractive choice for those whose children are less able. Some public schools use the TEACCH program, especially in North Carolina, where it originated.

RDI

Relationship Development Intervention (RDI) is a new early intervention approach, created by Houston psychologist Dr. Steven Gutstein. It incorporates some elements of ABA, but its special focus is on helping your child develop the ability to build relationships. Because it's new it hasn't been well studied, but one preliminary report suggests that it may be beneficial. I like the emphasis on relationship, but I'm concerned that the ABA elements may not be intensive enough to be appropriate for children with autism. But RDI could be an acceptable choice for a relatively high functioning child with Asperger syndrome. RDI is offered throughout childhood, rather than exclusively as an early intervention approach, so you could also complete your child's ABA and then begin an RDI program to improve his social skills. RDI practitioners are available in many locations, and some will travel to you to help you set up a program.[3]

FLOORTIME

Dr. Stanley Greenspan, a Washington, D.C., child psychiatrist, created the Floortime[4] approach. Like RDI, Floortime emphasizes improving your child's ability to form relationships. Unlike ABA, it doesn't contain any skills training. It hasn't been studied for effectiveness, so it must be considered unproven, however promising it sounds. Like RDI, it could be an acceptable choice for high-functioning Asperger kids. Many autism treatment centers and public school early intervention programs incorporate elements from the Floortime approach.

NEURODEVELOPMENTAL PATTERNING

Neurodevelopmental patterning is based upon the ideas of the late Drs. Glen Doman and Carl Delacato. These doctors developed a theory of brain development in the 1960s, which initially was enthusiastically received as promising, but was never proven to be effective by independent studies. Relatives trained by Drs. Doman and Delacato have kept their ideas alive in the United States and the United Kingdom, respectively. Treatment offered by organizations like the National Academy of Child Development (NACD) and their Christian spin-off, the International Christian Association of Neurodevelopmentalists (ICAN), have become popular among the homeschool community in the United States.

The American Academy of Pediatrics Committee on Children with Disabilities took the fairly unusual step of publishing a position paper condemning this approach in the 1980s.

> This treatment is based upon an outmoded and oversimplified theory of brain development. Current information does not support the claims of proponents that this treatment is efficacious, and its use continues to be unwarranted. . . . AAP concludes that patterning treatment continues to offer no special merit, that the claims of its advocates remain unproven, and that the demands and expectations placed on families are so great that in some cases their financial resources may be depleted substantially and parental and sibling relationships could be stressed.[5]

The American Academy of Pediatrics reaffirmed this policy statement in May 2006, so it's reasonable to conclude that the concerns they addressed in the earlier paper continue to be an issue. I'm unable to recommend this program.

SON-RISE

The Son-Rise approach is based upon the personal theories of Barry and Samahria Kaufman, who have no training in autism treatment. The organization offering the Son-Rise approach is the Autism Treatment Center of America, formerly known as the Options Institute. The foundational principle of this treatment is that you should offer what the Kaufmans call "unconditional acceptance" of your child. So, for example, to build a relationship with him, if he is stimming, you should join him in doing so. It's not clear how this enables a child to learn new skills or even to build a relationship. This treatment is completely untested, and raises concerns similar to those of the neurodevelopmental approach. I'm unable to recommend this program.

WHAT ABOUT SUPPLEMENTARY TREATMENTS?

A number of treatments have been developed that can be used as supplements to a good ABA program. These include various diets, medical treatments, vision, hearing, and sensory treatments.[6] It is important to recognize that, however dramatic the claims are that a particular approach can offer the hope of a "cure," if you pursue any of these approaches exclusively, without an ABA program, it's much less likely that your child will make striking gains. The best window of opportunity for your child to improve significantly is through ABA treatment during the early intervention years. Once that window is closed, the likelihood of improvement becomes less with each passing year. So if you want to pursue some of these other treatments at the same time as your child receives ABA, by all means do so. I certainly did. But I don't recommend that you pin all of your hopes on them.

APPENDIX C

Eric's
VALEDICTORIAN SPEECH

SO, WE ARE FINALLY GRADUATING. This perhaps means we've learned something worthwhile. What have we learned over the years here at Covenant? We have learned to read and write, to diagram sentences, to solve algebraic equations. Most importantly, we have studied the Bible in depth. We know that there is one God, who created everything and is Lord of the whole world. We are made in the image of this wise, all-powerful Creator. It is through God that we have our purpose, which is to glorify Him and to do His work.

Since this is true, the ultimate question must be, how do we glorify God, and what is His work? Is there one ideal personality type and set of abilities that glorifies God best? Is there one occupation that is "holier," a specific work that pleases God more than the others? Do we have to fit a mold? On the contrary, there is great diversity among human beings, and the Bible teaches that each of us is uniquely designed for the contribution that God intends us to make through our lives. Variety in human personality and talent glorifies God in the same way that variety in nature testifies to His wisdom and power.

But as we have grown into adults, each one of us has had to come to terms, in some way or another, not only with what gifts God has given us, but also with what He has not. None of us is everything that we dreamed we'd be when we were small. Some of us were disappointed when we did not grow as tall, or as big, as we wished to. Others of us might have preferred to be smaller. Some of us wanted to be smarter, or more creative, handsome, or beautiful than we turned out to be. Probably most of us wish we were more popular.

I was born with a serious handicap. And although I am truly grateful to God for enabling me to overcome most of the serious consequences of this condition, I must admit that I have often been tempted to ask, "Why can't I be more like everyone else?" This is when I must consciously remind myself of the truth that my life is not a mistake. God designed me JUST THE WAY I AM, and He has a purpose for me even in the things about me that are different. Perhaps especially in the things about me that are different. I have to make a conscious choice to believe what God's Word says is true about me, rather than believing what the world says about my value and importance.

Our society sets an exacting standard of achievement for us. If we don't fit the mold, we are—if not worthless—at least not important. If we do not have a high-paying job, if we do not drive a fancy car, if we do not have a beautiful wife and family, if we have not made a monumental scientific discovery, if we are not great athletes, if we are not admired and popular, then we don't matter. And those of us who have little potential to achieve in any of these areas are less than irrelevant. But this is not a biblical concept.

In Matthew 25, Jesus teaches in the parable of the talents that what we have been given is not as important as what we do with what we have been given. God is glorified when we place Him first in our lives and seek to use whatever gifts He has given us in service of His kingdom. In Luke 21, Jesus teaches us that the widow who put two small copper coins in the offering box put in more than anyone else, because she gave everything she had. He did not devalue her worth as a human being, even though the society of His time deemed her unimportant because she was a woman, a widow, and poor.

All of us, whether athletically gifted, intellectually superior, artistically talented, or compassionate "people persons," can be encouraged by the biblical truth that God has created each of us just the way we are for His glory and purpose. He is glorified as we each work for His kingdom in our own unique way to the best of our ability. If we do, on the last day He will say to us, "Well done, good and faithful servant."

Ultimately, our lives have meaning and purpose not because of our gifts or our accomplishments, but because of our relationship with the Lord Jesus

Christ. As we go forth into our adult lives, let us dedicate ourselves to finding what work He has especially suited us to do, purposing to seek His glory, rather than our own, in everything we do. Let us do our work with the goal of conforming ourselves to the image of Christ and pleasing Him, rather than conforming ourselves to the world's standard and pleasing ourselves. Let us continue faithful to the end, advancing Christ's kingdom through His grace and power. And may God enable us to glorify Him as we do so.

I want to thank each and every one of our guests for coming today to celebrate our graduation. Thank you, Mr. McManus, for being our principal for the past six years, and for leading each of us and touching our lives. Thank you, Pastor Wagner, for sacrificing your time by coming here daily to teach our Bible class, and for preaching at our chapel meetings. To all the staff and faculty who have worked with us over the years, I am deeply grateful. I want to thank my classmates, my fellow travelers, for being kind to me and being my friends. I also would like to thank my parents for carefully and patiently raising me, and for loving me. But most of all, I thank God for saving me and for delivering me through many hardships. It is only because of Him that I stand here today.

Glossary
OF TERMS

ABA (Applied Behavioral Analysis)
    An early intervention technique for autism, in which skills are taught in small, more easily mastered steps.

ASD (Autism Spectrum Disorder)
    A group of developmental challenges including autism and related diagnoses, including Asperger Syndrome and Pervasive Developmental Disorder (PDD). The terms ASD, autism, and PDD are often used interchangeably. Many doctors group autism and Asperger Syndrome together and refer to them jointly as ASDs. This is the terminology used in this book.

Able, more or less
    Referring to a child as "more able" or "less able" describes his abilities with respect to others on the autism spectrum. Children with ASDs can range from gifted to profoundly mentally challenged. Used interchangeably with "high (or low) functioning." (See Functioning, high or low.)

Accommodations

Refers to the help that the law entitles a person with a developmental challenge to receive, to help him participate in school or society.

Asperger Syndrome

A milder form of autism, which is one of the diagnoses on the milder end of the autism spectrum. This term is often used interchangeably with "high functioning autism." (See Functioning, high or low.)

Aspie

A nickname for individuals with Asperger Syndrome.

Autism Spectrum

Describes a group of related developmental challenges that include autism. (See ASD.)

Aversive

A behavioral term for negative or painful consequences that are used by a behaviorist to modify behavior. The use of aversives in a special education classroom are controversial and generally not recommended. Spanking, administered at home by a loving parent, is not considered an aversive.

BCBA (Board Certified Behavior Analyst)

An autism treatment professional, possessing at least a master's degree, trained to analyze an autistic child's behavior. Because he understands why the child behaves as he does, a BCBA can devise means to modify behavior.

Behaviorist

(See BCBA.)

Deficit

A medical term describing autism spectrum challenges in terms of what the child is unable to do. This is not the best way to understand an autism spectrum behavior. (See chapter 3.)

Drill

A behavioral term referring to a skill that is being taught in an ABA treatment program. Each repetition of the same drill is referred to as a trial. (See Trial.)

Early Intervention

Treatment that teaches verbal and other skills that have not yet been acquired by an autism spectrum child. Typically, early intervention begins before age four and ends with entry into kindergarten.

Fade

Special assistance that has been given to enable an autism spectrum child master a skill is slowly withdrawn as the child demonstrates the ability to perform the skill without help. The process of withdrawing the help is referred to as "fading."

Floortime

A non-ABA early intervention technique. See appendix B for details.

Functioning, high or low

A term used to compare the abilities of an autism spectrum individual with others who have the same diagnosis. Used interchangeably with "more (or less) able." (See Able, more or less.)

Inclusion

A special education term describing the degree to which an autism spectrum child is included in activities offered to general education students.

Mainstream

A special education term used to describe a challenged child who attends regular classes with general education students, rather than in a special education classroom.

Meltdown

A term that originated in the autism spectrum community to refer to autism spectrum tantrums. Although this term has become popular among parents, and is now commonly used to refer to any child's tantrum, the term first gained popularity because it captured the very severe and protracted nature of ASD tantrums. See chapter 6 for more information on meltdowns.

Neurotypical

A term used to distinguish autism spectrum children from those who do not have a developmental challenge. A neurotypical (or "typical") child is one who does not carry an ASD diagnosis.

Obsession

A thought or behavior that a child with an ASD becomes preoccupied with, to the exclusion of other interests.

Processing

A neurological term that describes the speed of brain functions. People with ASDs may have slower processing that makes keeping up with social interactions and classroom activities more difficult.

Prompt

A behavioral term for an instruction that calls for a response. For example, "Say 'cat'" is a prompt, calling for the response, "Cat."

Pullout

A special education term for a special activity, like speech or occupational therapy, which takes place in a mainstream (general education) classroom. A special education student is "pulled out" of his regular class to attend the activity.

RDI

Relationship Development Intervention. A non-ABA early intervention treatment. See appendix B for details.

Redirect

A behavioral term for drawing a child away from an undesirable activity by capturing his attention with a new activity.

Reward

A behavioral term for the positive consequence offered for successful performance of a drill. Rewards can include applause, effusive praise, or a small food treat. Rewards are commonly faded once the new behavior is established. (See Fade.)

Ritual

A behavior that an autism spectrum child may habitually perform, which seems to decrease anxiety. An autism spectrum ritual is usually performed the same way every time, and an autistic child may melt down if his ritual is interfered with.

Shadow

A behavioral term for the process of watching an autism spectrum child closely while prepared to intervene to prevent undesirable behaviors, or help him practice desired behaviors. The term is also sometimes used as a noun to refer to someone who is engaged in the process of shadowing a child.

Sheltered Work

A special education term that refers to work that a developmentally challenged adult does with the support of other, nonchallenged adults who assist him. Sheltered workshops enable individuals who would not otherwise be employable to hold a job.

Stim

Autism spectrum slang for self-stimulation. Individuals with ASDs commonly engage in a variety of behaviors that appear to soothe them and decrease anxiety. The term is used as a noun, to describe self-stimulating behavior, or as a verb, to describe the act of engaging in the behavior.

Spectrum

A nickname used to designate individuals on the autism spectrum. (See ASD and Autism Spectrum.)

Special Interest

Often used as a respectful way to refer to something that an autism spectrum individual is obsessed with. I use it in this book to describe the end result of successfully modifying an obsessional interest. A special interest may become the foundation for a rewarding career. (See chapter 8.)

Trial

A behavioral term referring to an individual repetition of a drill. (See Drill.)

Typical

An autism spectrum term used to refer to those who are not diagnosed with an ASD. Shorthand for "neurotypical." (The term carries less baggage than "normal," which implies that people on the autism spectrum are "abnormal.")

Notes

Chapter 1: In His Way

1. "Baby Mine," lyrics by Ned Washington, music by Frank Churchill, in *Dumbo*, directed by Ben Sharpsteen, Walt Disney Pictures, 1941.

2. The Council for Exceptional Children defines Autism Spectrum Disorder (ASD) as "an increasingly popular term that refers to a broad definition of autism including the classical form of the disorder as well as closely related disabilities that share many of the core characteristics. ASD includes the following diagnoses and classifications:

    (a) Pervasive Developmental Disorder—Not Otherwise Specified (PDD-NOS), which refers to a collection of features that resemble autism but may not be as severe or extensive;

    (b) Rett's syndrome, which affects girls and is a genetic disorder with hard neurological signs, including seizures, that become more apparent with age;

    (c) Asperger syndrome, which refers to individuals with autistic characteristics but relatively intact language abilities, and;

    (d) Childhood Disintegrative Disorder, which refers to children whose development appears normal for the first few years, but then regresses with the loss of speech and other skills until the characteristics of autism are conspicuous. Although the classical form of autism can be readily distinguished from other forms of ASD, the terms autism and ASD are often used interchangeably.

Individuals with autism and ASD vary widely in ability and personality. Individuals can exhibit severe mental retardation or be extremely gifted in their intellectual and academic accomplishments. While many individuals prefer isolation and tend to withdraw from social contact, others show high levels of affection and enjoyment in social situations. Some people with autism appear lethargic and slow to respond, but others are very active and seem to interact constantly with preferred aspects of their environment." www.cec.sped. org/AM/Template.cfm?Section=Home&TEMPLATE=/CM/ContentDisplay.cfm& CONTENTID=5690

To learn more about the characteristics of autism spectrum disorders, please turn to appendix A: "Is My Child on the Autism Spectrum?"

Chapter 2: First Steps in the Way

1. *Rain Man*, directed by Barry Levinson, MGM Studios, 1988.

Chapter 3: Shepherding the Heart of Your Child

1. Tedd Tripp, *Shepherding a Child's Heart* (Wapwollopen, PA: Shepherd Press, 1995). This book is highly recommended for general principles for nurturing all of our children, spectrum and typical.

2. Adapted from *Withhold Not Correction* by Bruce Ray (Phillipsburg, NJ: P&R Publishing, 1978), 88–91, which contains a discussion of how to discipline typical kids.

Chapter 4: Educating the Mind of Your Child

1. See, for example, Deuteronomy 28.

2. I highly recommend Tedd Tripp's *Shepherding a Child's Heart* (Wapwollopen, PA: Shepherd Press, 1995). It teaches general principles for nurturing all of our children, spectrum and typical. Please note that this wonderful book does make negative comments about what Dr. Tripp calls "behaviorism." By this he means using "bribes" as a child training and management tool for typical children. Dr. Tripp's point is that parents need to understand what's going on inside their child as they address his misbehavior, rather than just using techniques to make him behave without concerning themselves with his attitudes. I couldn't agree more with Dr. Tripp on this point, and I don't think he intends to preclude the temporary use of behavioral techniques to train developmentally delayed children. But Dr. Tripp's caution bears careful attention. If we as autism spectrum parents keep our focus on shaping behavior with rewards once our children are functioning more typically, we may fail to "get to the heart" of our child's misbehavior.

3. J. J. McEachin, T. Smith, and O. I. Lovaas, "Long-term Outcome for Children with Autism Who Received Early Intensive Behavioral Treatment," *American Journal on Mental Retardation* 97 (1993): 359–72.

4. If you are interested in this option, check out www.nathhan.com, the Web site of the National Challenged Homeschoolers Associated Network. Some of these parents are homeschooling several challenged and multicapped children at the same time. They offer a wealth of experience, resources, and encouragement.

Chapter 5: Stims, Rituals, and Obsessions

1. Watty Piper, *The Little Engine That Could* (New York: Grosset & Dunlap, 1978).

2. Tony Attwood, *Asperger's Syndrome: A Guide for Parents and Professionals* (London: Jessica Kingsley Publishers, 1998), 89–102.

3. Bill Bryson, *Notes from a Small Island* (New York: Harper-Collins, 1998), 219.

Chapter 6: Managing Emotions

1. Tony Attwood, *The Complete Guide to Asperger Syndrome*, (London: Jessica Kingsley Publishers, 2007), 143.

2. Tony Attwood, *Exploring Feelings: Cognitive Behaviour Therapy to Manage Anxiety, Sadness, and Anger* DVD, Arlington TX: Future Horizons, Inc., 2007.

3. Carol Gray, *Comic Strip Conversations* (Arlington TX: Future Education, 1994).

4. I contributed several chapters on special-needs kids to *When Good Kids Make Bad Choices*, by Elyse Fitzpatrick and Jim Newheiser (Eugene, OR: Harvest House 2003). The book contains a fuller discussion of the uses of psychiatric medicines in kids, and contains an appendix listing common side effects of medicines in common use.

5. *Proverbs for Parenting* by Barbara Decker (Boise, ID: Lynn's Bookshelf, 1995) is a topical list of Bible verses that are pertinent to child raising. Highly recommended!

6. Two of the best I've found are *Getting a Grip: The Heart of Anger Handbook for Teens*, by Lou Priolo (Merrick, NY: Calvary Press, 2006), and *The Young Peacemaker* by Corlette Sande (Wapwallopen, PA: Shepherd Press, 1997). *Getting a Grip* is best for older teens, while *Young Peacemaker* is presented in a winsome, comic-book style that hits the mark perfectly for younger, or lower-functioning kids.

Chapter 7: The Relationship Puzzle

1. Liane Holliday Willey, *Pretending to Be Normal* (New York: Jessica Kingsley Publishers, 1999), 17.

2. Judy and Sean Barron, *There's a Boy in Here* (Arlington, TX: Future Horizons, 2002), 113.

3. You can learn more about Temple Grandin's work and publications at www.templegrandin.com.

4. Quoted in Tony Attwood, *The Complete Guide to Asperger's Syndrome* (Philadelphia: Jessica Kingsley Publishers, 2007), 58.

5. Mr. Spock and Lt. Data were nonhuman characters who didn't understand human ways, in the *Star Trek* television programs in the 1960s and 1980s, respectively. Lt. Data was a particularly poignant character in his desire to be more like humans and experience human love.

6. To find some of these, you can search the phrase "neurotypical disorder." I found this to be an empathy-building experience!

Chapter 8: Mad Elephants and Maturity

1. Temple Grandin has authored a book on careers for autism spectrum people that takes this general approach to turning interests and talents into job opportunities. It's called *Developing Talents: Careers for Individuals with Asperger Syndrome and High Functioning Autism*, by Temple Grandin and Kate Duffy (Shawnee Mission KS: Autism Asperger Publishing, 2004). I highly recommend this resource. You can find it at www.futurehorizons-autism.com.

2. Private schools for developmentally challenged adults, your local regional center, public school, or department of rehabilitation may be able to help you find such community resources. The *Autism Advocate*, a publication of the Autism Society of America, devoted an issue to work issues for autism spectrum adults (First Edition 2007, volume 46, no. 1). You can find the Autism Society of America at www.autism-society.org.

3. Information about Temple's childhood comes from her mother's autobiography, *A Thorn in My Pocket*, by Eustacia Cutler (Arlington, TX: Future Horizons, 2004).

4. You can learn more about how and why the squeeze chute helps Temple in Oliver Sacks, *An Anthropologist on Mars* (New York: Vintage Books, 1995), 262–5.

5. Ibid.

6. You can read more about Temple's views about her brain uniqueness in Temple Grandin, *Thinking in Pictures* (New York: Vintage Books, 1995).

7. You can read more about Temple's humane slaughterhouse designs and why they work in Dr. Sacks's chapter on Temple in *An Anthropologist on Mars*, 244–96. Also see http://grandin. com/professional.resume.html and http://en.wikipedia.org/wiki/Slaughterhouse.

8. You can view these documentaries at www.stephenwiltshire.co.uk/documentaries. aspx.

9. You can view some of Stephen's work at www.stephenwiltshire.co.uk/gallery.aspx.

10. Sacks, *An Anthropologist on Mars*, 213.

11. You can view it at www.youtube.com/watch?v=erFriz9HNMg. (If the video doesn't come up, type Autism Employment in the search; Jonathan's story is tagged "A short video featuring my brother on people with Autism in the workplace. . . ." It's well worth watching!)

Chapter 9: For This Child I Prayed

1. First Samuel 1:24 tells us that Hannah took Samuel to Shiloh after she'd weaned him. He would have been about three years old.

2. The family's customary visit to Shiloh happened once a year (1 Samuel 1:3). After Samuel went to live in Shiloh, the Bible tells us that the family continued this practice (1 Samuel 2:19). Although there could have been other visits, they couldn't have been very frequent, because of the distance involved.

3. See the story in 1 Samuel 3:2–18, where Samuel was given a prophecy by the Lord. The Bible doesn't tell us if Eli, the high priest, was also sleeping in the temple, or in his own tent nearby. But Samuel had to "run to Eli" (verses 5, 6, and 8), which tells us that wherever Eli was, Samuel was sleeping alone.

Appendix A: "Is My Child on the Autism Spectrum?"

1. Cited in Lorna Wing, *The Autistic Spectrum*, (Berkeley: Ulysses Press, 2001), 12. Chapter 3 of this book contains a very comprehensive description of typical autism spectrum behaviors, and is highly recommended.

2. *Rain Man*, directed by Barry Levinson, MGM Studios, 1988.

3. Families of Adults Affected by Asperger Syndrome (FAAAS) is a support group for spouses and parents of adult children. You can visit their Web site at http://faaas.org. There are a number of books on marriage to Asperger spouses. I am not able to give an unqualified recommendation for any of them, but links from the FAAAS Web site will lead you to several of them.

Appendix B: Selecting a Treatment Program

1. You can find the Lovaas Institute online at www.lovaas.com.

2. You can find information online at www.teacch.com.

3. You can find RDI online at www.rdiconnect.com.

4. You can find Floortime online at www.floortime.org.

5. You can read this position paper in its entirety at http://aappolicy.aappublications.org/cgi/content/full/pediatrics;104/5/1149.

6. If you're interested in learning more about these treatments, *Facing Autism* by Lynn M. Hamilton (Colorado Springs: Waterbrook, 2000) is a helpful resource that offers a brief overview on many of these, written by a Christian autism spectrum mother who used both ABA and supplementary treatments.

WILL MEDICINE STOP THE PAIN?

Twice as many women as men will experience depression sometime
in their lives. Many of these women are given medication to treat the
disease, but medication alone does not address the underlying
emotions that trouble the mind and spirit. Fitzpatrick and
Hendrickson provide biblical guidance on how to balance medical
intervention with biblical encouragement.

 MOODY
PUBLISHERS.

1-800-678-8812 · MOODYPUBLISHERS.COM